G000075674

Long

A BWWM Sweet & Steamy Romance

By

Stella Eromonsere-Ajanaku

A Flirty & Feisty Romance Novel

...Love for real

Sexy Teaser

"I thought I'd get over the way I felt in one day. In the last few days, all I've wanted was to see you, to talk to you, to kiss you. Once wasn't enough, Kiarra."

Twisting her mouth, she hovered her eyes around his attractive lips.

"Did you have fun at the barbecue party, Ryder?"

"No. You weren't there, so it wasn't the same."

His tone had a rough edge, he almost sounded like he missed her. But she found that hard to believe.

"I'm not the life of the party, Ryder."

"Everyone thinks I'm the reason you didn't show."

To avoid replying, she reached for the kettle. From her side, Ryder covered her hand with his own.

Gasping, she dragged in a long breath.

"Take your hands off. I want to make coffee."

"Not until you tell me why you're running away from me. You kissed me back with enough passion to light up this entire country. That kind of passion doesn't fade away in one week for no reason."

Her pulse jumped all over the place and her heart thudded. *"You've not given me one reason to stay."*

Coals burned up her arms. Heat scalded her cleavage and left her nipples raw with need. Night after night, she had longed for his touch and his kisses. Even now standing so close, she trembled.

"Don't run away from me, from us," he whispered stroking the back of her hand.

"There's no us. I can't do this with you, Ryder."

"Why not?"

Longing for You

This book is a work of fiction. All names, characters and events in this publication, other than those clearly in the public domain, are fictitious and any resemblance to real persons, living or dead, is purely coincidental.

Praise

Book #32 is published.

Great God, the King above all gods who dwells in Heaven, I bow before you in gratitude. I thank you for Jesus Christ my Saviour, my Rock, my inspiration and my strength.

I give you all the glory, Lord Jesus for your unfailing love and for your wonderful deeds for me, my family and for the world. Thank you for giving me strength in my weakness to write, to publish and for all my readers you send to read my books.

To you be all the glory, honour and praise, forever, Amen.

Sincere Gratitude

I love you forever, the love of my life and my honey-boo. You've been a blessing to me and our wonderful children. May our joy overflow always and may the Lord honour and lead you in all your ways.

My amazing two grown-up kids, I love you to the moon and back, forever. May the Lord bless, favour, honour and guide you always.

Thank you to my parents, brothers and sisters, especially to you, my Aize dearest, huge thanks for supporting me and for loving me without a doubt. I love you, baby girl. May God favour you all and your families.

To my supporters and readers who take it upon themselves to share and promote my books on their pages, I'm super grateful. You are all blessed.

Every reader of **Flirty & Feisty Romance Novels** across the world is precious to me. Thank you so much for checking, buying and reading my books. I'm ecstatic knowing you bought each book. I hope you love reading *Longing for You* as much as I loved writing every word.

When you leave a review, I get butterflies in my stomach. I love you all. God bless you.

Books by Stella

Flirty & Feisty Contemporary and Interracial Romance:

Longing for You

Irresistible Driver

Get Undressed

Christmas Desire

Tempted by the Princess – Book 1

Tempted by the Princess – Book 2

Hooked by one Curvy Girl – Book 1

Hooked by one Curvy Girl – Book 2

Naughty Promise

Christmas Seduction

Irresistible Passion

"Shocking Affair"

Guilty of Love

Your Christmas Gift

All of Me

"You're Mine"

Enticed Forever

Naked Attraction

Indecent

His Ring

Forbidden Dance (Forbidden Series #1)

Red Velvet Rose (Forbidden Series #2)

Tempting Desire

Seduced Hearts

Lust

Stolen Kisses (Books 1 & 2)

Wild Whispers

Love at Christmas

Husband to Rent

Stolen Valentine Kiss (Holiday Series #1)

Kiss My Lips (Holiday Series #2)

Royal Cowries (Cowries Series #1)

His Choice (Cowries Series #2)

A Bit About Me

I'm Stella Eromonsere-Ajanaku, born and raised in the ancient Benin City of Nigeria, West Africa. My birth city has a monarchy that is over 6000years old. But I now live in London, UK with my husband, and our two grown-ups.

To be honest, nothing thrills me more than to write sizzling romance novels that have intriguing and captivating plots which boast compelling characters who have hearts and souls and jump off the pages.

The stories are dotted with unexpected twists and are set in fascinating Africa, enticing Europe and enchanting America & Canada. If you need a novel to knock off the stress of daily living, cure you of boredom, make you laugh, keep you drooling in suspense and draw you into an intensely emotional spin, pick up one of mine to read. They have a high entertainment value.

In 2010, I created *Flirty & Feisty Romance Novels*.

To experience an emotional ride with my characters, just cuddle up, grab a copy of *Flirty & Feisty Romance Novels* and sail away to Pleasure Island. I will love to hear from you.

Dear Reader,

Have you met anyone who proposed to a total stranger? I hadn't until I wrote *Longing for You*.

If someone had told Kiarra Wright she would propose to a guy she just met, she would have yelled a harsh, *no!* But she did. And he turned her down.

For good reasons, she shows up again in his condo. Adamant he wants nothing to do with her, Ryder Blade asks her to leave. She doesn't.

Attracted by her curvy appeal and more, he sees layers of the woman no other guy knows about.

Then his own flaws pop up.

Now he wants her...

But it's too late.

She has walked out of his life.

You must read *Longing for You* to find out if Ryder will forgo his pride to get a chance at love with Kiarra, and if she will give him a second chance.

If you have not read any of my **32** other sizzling romance novels, please start now.

If you have any comments, please write to Stella at *Authorstella@gmail.com*

Hugs & Love,
Stella Eromonsere-Ajanaku

Praise for Stella's Books

Longing for You: "I absolutely loved this story! Highly recommend it to all hopeful romantics out there! The experiences this couple went through was very realistic. Ready for this author's next read!"
~ *Rated 5stars by LadyTee89.*

Irresistible Driver: "A very good steamy read! ...In the end, love conquers all. This author never disappoints. Her flirty romances are absolutely the best!" ~ *Rated 5stars by LadyTee89.*

Get Undressed: "Very different type of match making...to go outside their boundaries to find true love. Enjoyed this couples journey to their HEA."
~ *Rated 4stars by Mae Dixon.*

Christmas Desire: "Such a lovely tale! That element of surprise really got me. I loved the characters. Eboni and Jensen intrigued me."
~ *Rated 5stars by LadyTee89.*

Tempted by the Princess: "Oh my goodness... I love this story. It's a feel good, getaway, relaxing on the beach, or in a soothing bubble bath type of story. Declan and Kahina are FIRE..."
~ *Rated 5stars by Kindle Customer.*

Hooked by one Curvy Girl – Book 1: "Sweet & sexy story...Amara and Brad seems so right for each other but both are afraid that secrets can ruin their love. He wants what she cannot give..."
~ *Rated 5 stars by KittyOh48.*

Hooked by one Curvy Girl – Book 2: "This hot romance read series ended on an excellent note... These two needed each other... A lovely story! A love inspired story with God's timing and grace - a happily ever after!" ~ *Rated 5 stars by LadyTee89*

Naughty Promise: "This was a very dear story to me. Kemi and Clifton had me in tears. I didn't want it to end. It was an emotional read. They both tried to fight their irresistibly attraction... But true love conquers all. I truly loved this story."
~ Rated 5 stars by LadyTee89.

CHRISTMAS Seduction: "...I do have to say that once you start reading this book you won't be able to put it down. This book made my day extremely joyous." ~ *Rated 5 stars by Kindle Customer.*

IRRESISTIBLE Passion: "I totally loved this story from the beginning to the end. What an exceptional read .... The relationships between Jayden and Tiana was so sweet I totally feel in love with their lives." ~ *Rated 5 stars by Gloria J Hill.*

""Shocking Affair": I loved this! ...When the chemistry is so strong between two souls, no amount of interference from those who don't feel the same is enough to keep this pair apart. I love this book...""
~ Rated 5 stars by LadyTee89.

Guilty of Love – "This was a very hot and steamy tale! The interaction between the characters was so realistic...and were so unpredictable I couldn't put the book down until I finished!" ~ *Rated 5 stars by nina.*

Your Christmas Gift – "Oh what a great quick read and a sweet story! It is great from the first page to the last...

I do so LOVE your books! Please keep them coming." ~ *Rated 5 stars by LHill.*

All of Me – "I adored this story... The characters were sexy, hilarious and so real! This story had me at page 1...great read! ❤"
~ *Rated 5 stars by Readyreader.*

"You're Mine" – I enjoyed this book from the beginning so very much!! Meeting sassy Rachael and the very alpha Banjo was so amazing! Such a well-written story that is so unique and lovely!! Brought tears to my eyes..." ~ *Rated 5 stars by Rhonda Adels.*

Husband to Rent – "I have to say the chemistry that Stella Eromonsere-Ajanaku characters have in these books, make me want to move into one of her books, so I can find my King."
~ *Rated 5 stars by georgiana braham.*

"**Enticed Forever** has a great storyline and the chemistry between Theo and Aize hooked me right into their story and kept me totally enthralled until the very end!" ~ *Rated 5 stars by Pat W.*

"In **Naked Attraction**...The images that play in my mind as I read about locations, foods and situations seem as if I'm watching a movie. The way she describes the characters and their chemistry is awesome.... I recommend it."
~ *Rated 5 stars by ReadyReader.*

His Ring: *"*Truly loved this story. It's such a sweet love story to read!! I fell in love with Yomi and the story itself held my attention to the very end. I laughed, I cried and I loved the ending!!!"
~ *Rated 5 stars by Layla Morgan.*

His Choice: "What a beautifully written love story. A prince who has his heart set on a woman he cannot have with a very interesting twist I enjoyed so much, I could not put the book down until I finished..." ~ *Rated 5 stars by amazon customer.*

"Lust: This was such a wonderful story! I loved the relationship that grew between Jordan and Faye... I cried, I laughed and I didn't want to put it down."
~ *Rated 5 stars by amazon customer*

Love at Christmas: "...Stella is a writer who draws you into the story and her characters. It was a pleasure to read... It made me feel emotional and as if Christmas was already here."
~ *Rated 5 stars by Lisa Caddick*

"Stolen Valentine Kiss–I enjoyed the romance story that developed from a lingering look. I loved how two hearts became one and there were moments that I was scared. Lorna and Logan are perfect for each other..." ~ *Rated 5 stars by Deborah Brandon.*

Kiss My Lips – "What a great escape for me. Logan is...sweet, sensitive, thoughtful, everything that we would look for in a book boyfriend. This was a great read from start to finish."
~ *Rated 5 stars by avid reader.*

"Royal Cowries – This novel is like the movies Queenie, Roots and Shaka Zulu with a more modern way of thinking, surviving, love...within a passionate love story. Excellent!!!" ~ *Rated 5 stars by T. Miles*

"**Forbidden Dance** is a breath-taking romance novel... The reader is taken on a whirlwind affair filled with pleasure, lust, sensuality, desire and sweltering sex. A well-written, remarkable page-turning read."

~ *Rated 5 stars by Vivienne Diane Neal.*

"**Tempting Desire,** I thoroughly enjoyed reading this novel. I was hooked from the very first page. The story line was so real I could visualise each of the characters. It was as if I was watching a life movie."

~ *Rated 5 stars by Amazon Customer.*

"**Seduced Hearts:** Outstanding book! Excellent read. It's so nuanced, it sparkles. It's definitely worth reading!" ~ *Rated 5 stars by Russell Mebane.*

Red Velvet Rose: "This novel is a masterpiece, I couldn't stop reading until I finished the book..."

~ *Rated 5 stars by Itohan.*

"**Wild Whispers:** Wild whispers is a beautiful story and...once I picked it up to read, I couldn't put it down until I got to the end... True love as discovered by Adaora and Gary is spontaneous and not bound by time or space." ~ *Rated 5stars by Gharriluc.*

Content

Chapter 1 – Cut The Crap

Kiarra

"Will you marry me?" Winking where she sat at a table for two, Kiarra Wright directed her deep brown gaze and cheeky question to the new entrant into the party circle.

Silence hung in the air for a second, or two. In the moment following the quiet, Kiarra lifted her wineglass and smiled.

"Not in a million years!" Ryder Blade responded without blinking his pensive hazel eyes.

Though she scoffed, Kiarra allowed his words to settle down. Maybe it was the sound of his voice, sharp and very deep that cluttered her senses.

The party size of six, excluding Kiarra and Ryder viewed the emerging feud with broad grins. Everyone there lived in various condos at *Cable Point*, the massive blue and white building along *Marquette Place* in San Diego, California.

One Saturday a month, they hung out at the secluded barbecue spot on the grounds of the building to chitchat. Lush green, soft rolling hills meandered around the extensive place, providing a scenic backdrop on a sun-friendly afternoon.

Meanwhile, the beer bottle in Ryder's hand pecked his lips–bordered by groomed beard. While he took a quick swig, his prominent Adam Apple jabbed at his round neck white T-shirt as he swallowed.

Shaking her shoulder-length, dark curls, Kiarra adjusted the spaghetti sleeves of her pale-blue, acid-wash denim dress. She was at least happy her sun kissed skin was on show in her knee-length outfit. Maybe she was crazy to call, Ryder out the way she had. But with the gloomy expression and mysterious air the guy wore like an armour how was she, or any woman expected to approach him?

"Why are you turning down my marriage proposal?" Kiarra countered moments later, rolling back her smooth-edged shoulders. "Is it because I'm not your type, or you think you're too good for the best black woman you've ever met, hmm?"

Where did her boldness come from? Kiarra asked herself the same question on everyone's mind. Apart from the quick jolts in her chest and the soft tingling in her belly, she was outwardly composed.

"I don't owe you an explanation, lady," Ryder flared, speaking through tight lips, his beer bottle swinging from side to side in his large hand.

"Wrong answer."

Standing tall at well over six feet, Ryder Blade shrugged his macho shoulders which would have been the perfect hot bed for any woman's work-weary head when needed. As his muscles stretched, her eyes went straight to his huge biceps straining against his unbuttoned denim shirt worn over his T-shirt and dark blue slim fit jeans.

"I don't care." His tone was abrupt.

Angular face boasted straight, long-tipped nose that suggested he never got into bar brawls. Trimmed at the sides and back, his dark brown hair–whipped to and fro into a messy faux hawk because of the light wind–added to his enigmatic demeanour.

"I think you do," Kiarra maintained after she was done eating her barbecue chicken wings, grilled potato and bacon skewers.

In Kiarra's opinion, any man with a sexiness that was off the charts had no right to put on a get-off-my-face mien. Being pleasant cost nothing.

"Just so we're clear, I'm not the marrying type. I've got no love to give to any woman. Period." Chest out, shoulders back, Ryder steadied his eyes on her.

Swiping one bronzed hand in the air, she persisted. "What happened to you? Someone cut out your heart and soul and burnt it before you moved in to *Cable Point Condos*?"

"Ouch!" Jamie whistled. Dark-skinned, dark-eyed he was always armed with a buzz haircut and a sense of humour. "The shield is off. Let the fight begin."

Others shook their heads in disagreement. No one else spoke up. But Kiarra was convinced there was something damaged about their new neighbour.

"Ladies, he's got no heart, or maybe some woman crushed it on his way to San Diego," Jason added his two cents guess after finger-combing his wheat-coloured fringe haircut while his nose coloured red from chuckling.

"Why don't you all find something, or someone else to talk about?" Ryder spat through clenched, even white teeth. "Let me have one beer and eat the barbecue chicken in peace."

Ryder angled his head as if winking at the sun. His cheeks, now lightly pink toned by the heat, lent colour to his ivory skin moulded on an otherwise granite square face.

After Kiarra swallowed her drink, she thrust one hand on her wide hip.

"But there's no peace on *Marquette Place in* San Diego. Didn't anyone tell you before you moved into our neighbourhood? We're in each other's business because we care. Our families are faraway. We've only got each other to lean on in this bustling city."

Averting his gaze, Ryder checked his gold wristwatch, an expensive-looking one, Kiarra noted.

"Don't lean on me," Ryder grunted. "I won't lean on anyone. That's a promise."

"OK. We need an explanation for your anti-social posture. You owe us that much." For some unknown reason, Kiarra was not ready to throw in the towel with the mysterious stranger.

"I don't owe you anything," was Ryder's comeback. "But let me say this, I moved in here for a slice of peace and productivity. That's what I want."

At that moment, Kiarra imagined she threw a punch at his straight nose, not just to bend it out of shape but to also wipe off the smug look on his sculptured features. Instead of a blow however, she opted to kill him with sweet words.

"That's not on, Ryder. We can't allow your attractive chest and shoulders–built to be a warm hideout for women in need–go to waste."

The six other people present at the barbecue party convulsed with laughter while Kiarra and Ryder locked eyes in a staring contest. The awareness contest lasted for over a minute. Neither of them gave in. The tension heightened even after they blinked.

"I nominate Kiarra Wright to show Ryder Blade the *Cable Point Condos* hospitality starting from tomorrow. If you support my idea, say yeah," Duane, a dark-skinned, five-feet-eleven guy trumpeted.

All six people present put up their hands and chorused an enthusiastic, "Yeah!"

Every time a new condo owner, or resident moved in to the building, a condo buddy was assigned to generally make life simpler for the occupant in a new environment, or a new city in some instances.

"There's no turning back now," Kiarra jeered crinkling her long, square-tipped nose at Ryder. "I'm afraid you're stuck with me, a bronzed, curvy woman who doesn't take bullshit from any guy."

Laughter circulated around the small group.

"I don't need this intrusion in my life!" he quipped unsmiling, stroking his groomed jaw, now hardened like it would soon crack.

Trying not to face the fact she was extra pushy to help because Ryder Blade was so damn good-looking and mysterious, Kiarra raised one dark, soft-angled eyebrow.

"Too bad. You're stuck with me as your condo buddy," she asserted with a winning grin.

"You might just unwind and have fun while Kiarra's making your life easier," Madison, the slim blonde told him. "Trust us, everyone needs someone to lean on at some point."

"I can attest to that," Nicole, a tall brunette tossed in her own affirmation. "When I first moved in here, I was withdrawn too, but the people here made settling down a whole lot easier for me. Besides, these monthly barbecue parties offer a great opportunity to laugh, tease one another, enjoy each other's company and catch up."

"In your dreams, ladies," came Ryder's flat reply through slightly closed fine lips.

Nothing anyone said dented his resolve to remain closed off.

"Whoever has ruined your emotions is to blame, not me, not Madison, or Nicole," Kiarra stressed, narrowing her eyes. "I'll do my best to make sure you know the rules, Ryder."

Maybe Kiarra's eagerness to help an unwilling newcomer stemmed from the fact some of the people around today helped her get through her rough start in a different city and neighbourhood when she first moved in a couple of years ago. Their help was invaluable.

Having only moved in a couple of weeks ago, no one knew whether, or not Ryder was new in San Diego.

Glancing sideways with an enigmatic smile shaping his lips, Ryder tossed back his beer in a final swig.

"In case you weren't listening earlier, I said I'm not here to fit in with your group. What part of that's so hard to understand, Kiarra?"

It was the first time he had called her by name all afternoon.

"All of it!" Duane came to Kiarra's defense. "Dude, chill. Be nice to the ladies."

"Look, no offense, I don't need friends, or a nosy neighbour sticking her nose in my personal life," Ryder insisted, his pointed-tipped nose flaring at the sides. "Respect my space and I'll respect yours."

Up on her feet now, Kiarra marched to stand next to Ryder. She cocked her head to peer up at him. Even in her three-inch blue denim wedge sandals, she only came up below his shoulder. Five-five was a good height for her if she were standing far from a lofty, Ryder Blade. The guy stood head and shoulders above everyone around.

"Step back." His hazel eyes blazed, turning a fierce gold shade.

"Cut the crap, Ryder!" Kiarra spat out finally losing her cool. "This is *Cable Point Condos,* San Diego, California. And, this is the way we do things here. If you don't like it, move out. We're not changing our ways for you. If you stay, it means you're going to be seeing more of me. Understood?"

"Whoa! That's the spirit, Kiarra!" the others roared. "Tell him how we do it here."

Chin up and flushed faced now, Ryder retorted. "Get off my back, Kiarra! Go get a life. Find a guy who's into your brand of friendship, or sexiness because I'm not."

"That's harsh!" Duane and Jamie said at once."

"Fortunately, I've not found any man whose brand of charm and sexiness I find appealing." Kiarra stabbed a finger at Ryder's bicep straining past his short-sleeve denim shirt. She ignored the zebra tattoos that morphed his arms into a show piece.

"Keep searching." The snide remark rolled off his tongue with ease.

"Sure. I won't look your way. You, on the other hand with your uneven edges and soulless chatter make for an interesting, yet cynical neighbour. Mark my words, you'll regret every word you've said today, I promise you, Ryder Blade."

But how can one guy have many attractive features? While she poked him with words, she glanced away from his in-your-face tattoos sheathing his veined forearms.

"I've got no time for this." Ryder's feet bumped one chair aside as he moved away from her. "Excuse me. I'm out of here. Don't follow me, Kiarra."

"Wasn't planning to follow you just yet, tough guy."

After Ryder exited, Madison and Nicole exchanged high fives with Kiarra.

"You've got thick skin, girl!" Madison praised. "That deliciously handsome guy needs you to shake his balls until he pleads for mercy."

The women split their sides laughing while the men stared at them wide-eyed.

"Ryder's uptight. Nothing a few massages can't fix," Nicole suggested. "Whoa! Those muscles—"

"No other woman can take that jerk's insult," Duane spat, interrupting Madison and Nicole drooling over a man who did not give a rat's ass. "The guy's a douche bag. Why did you sit there while he bashed you, Kiarra?"

"Did you doze off at the ring side, or something?" Monica, the last person to speak all afternoon asked with a wide grin. "Kiarra won the fight. She stood up to him and wiped off his smug look at the end. I saw and heard it all." The Brazilian, dark haired clapped for her champion. "I'm proud of you, girl."

"If you're on Team Kiarra after the fiasco that just ended, say yeah," Duane stated, asking for a vote.

"Yeah!" the women cheered along with Jamie.

"Nicole, Madison, Monica and Jamie. Four for Team Kiarra. Now, how many people for Team Ryder?" Madison mocked, snickering in Duane's face.

"Yeah," Jason and Duane voted in the minority.

They all laughed at the result.

"Despite what Ryder says, can't you see he's cold and empty inside?" Kiarra countered. "He's obviously got problems. Whatever he says, he needs us. Besides, I got a rise from watching him react. Way better than seeing his dark expression."

Jason nodded. "I see where you're coming from, Kiarra."

"I wanted to punch his nose a few times," Jamie mentioned in case anyone missed his silent inaction.

Laughter erupted from each person.

"No offense, Jamie, but I'm pretty sure, Ryder Blade would break your neck in a fist fight, or in any fight at all," Nicole contradicted.

Everyone knew Nicole had a thing for Jamie, but he had no clue.

"On this one, I agree with Madison," Kiarra voted, smiling, though her thoughts kept drifting back to the guy with muscles locked in a sculpted body and a voice like no other dude she had known. "Ryder looks ruthless on the outside. But he doesn't scare me."

"Maybe you should be scared after all," Jason gave his final verdict. "The way he acted today, the guy doesn't know how to treat a woman right. I don't want him to do anything stupid to you, Kiarra. Seriously."

"Hey! Let's not jump to hasty conclusions," Kiarra cautioned. "We don't know his back story. But I know one thing for sure, I can handle Ryder Blade anytime of the day."

Ryder

Thoroughly pissed at being called out by the dark, curly-haired woman with flashing eyes the colour of roasted coffee, Ryder power walked along the one-point-three miles route via *Kemper Street* to *Hancock Street Café*. The uninterrupted trek gave him plenty of time to work out his fury and to clear his head.

Once he sat on one of the seats under the parasol outside the café, and his drink and meal glared back at him, he took out his cell phone.

Right now, he needed to blow off steam. And he knew the person to call.

The moment Ryder pressed the call button, his friend, Jerrad Stone, one of California's accomplished plastic surgeon coughed in his ear.

"What the hell, bro?" Jerrad staged his response in a croaky voice.

"Are you alone?" Ryder was quick to respond. "Answering on the first ring isn't your style."

Jerrad was famous for answering calls after the fifth ring. It was a bad habit he refused to ditch.

"Knew it was you. What's up? You sound off."

"Remind me, why did I settle for *Cable Point Condos* again?"

His friend from pre-school chuckled, gloating at the other end. "What is it? You got a nightmare neighbour already?"

"That's right," Ryder confirmed with a nod. "One crazy woman is on my case, bro."

"What did she do that's so crazy?"

"In front of six people, the first thing out of her mouth at a barbecue party this afternoon was *will you marry me?*"

Jerrad whistled. "Wow! She's one wild oyster. Tell me she's easy on the eyes? Every good-looking woman deserves one pass at least."

"I don't care how easy she is on your eyes," Ryder snapped. "She's a huge pain in my ass and that's putting it mildly."

"Okay. I sense frustration. Does this nightmare neighbour have a name? Though I don't see how asking you to marry her is such a terrible thing, considering you're closer to forty than thirty."

"Kiarra Wright. Why are you concerned about her name anyway? Wait! I'm closer to forty? You were a lot closer to the big six zero before botox!"

Both men roared with laughter for a long minute.

"If Kiarra's good-looking, I suggest you hook up and be done with her. That should keep her quiet."

Letting out a long exhale, Ryder massaged his temple. "Sex doesn't solve every problem, bro. For once, just think outside the box."

"You know sex solves all our problems over here in Oceanfront Walk. I warned you about crossing over to the other side of San Diego. Women are feistier."

"You sound like I crossed state lines. I'm less than twenty-minutes' drive away."

"Anyhow it feels like you're out of the country. So, what do you want to do about our marriage-friendly Kiarra? Marry her and live happy ever after?"

Against his will, mirth blew up through Ryder's gut. He laughed knocking his elbow against the table edge.

"Are you stoned, J?"

"Nah. Had this chic in my house last night. She fucked my good brains out."

"I thought so. What was her name?"

"I'll ask her next time," Jerrad quipped.

"Where did you find her?"

"Where else? At the bar. There were two slender blondes last night. If you were here, you would've had your choice. The one I skipped reminded me of your booty caller, Hailey."

"Get a grip and grow up, J. We're not high schoolers anymore. At least ask for her name. You need to get married, have some kids and be done. That's what your parents expect."

"And you figure the names the sex-loving, money-grabbers give isn't fake? These women want a good time, not marriage. My parents will have to wait until I find my soulmate."

"Trust builds over time. Give one woman hope, J."

"Great advice from someone who's pissed off at a woman who has a name. What's wrong with Kiarra? Too short? Too fat?"

"Nothing is wrong with Kiarra," Ryder hurried to refute. "Did I say there was something wrong with her figure?"

"Wow! Rushing to defend her now? Who said anything about her figure? You were ready to kill her minutes ago. What? Is she gorgeous?"

Ryder waited more than a heartbeat to respond. In that interval, Kiarra's gusty gaze and confident attitude harassed his thoughts. Throughout their heated dialogue earlier, he had seen how the natural light brushed her bronzed skin so that her round arms and thick legs glowed like chocolate opal. Her dark brown eyes glimmered with emotion every time she opened her glossy, full lips. Even now, her rich, spice-loaded scent lingered on his shirt.

"Are you still there?" his friend asked. "Or did your thoughts float to Kiarra?"

"Shut up! Forget I ever mentioned her name."

"My bad. Your loss. If you change your mind, fuck Kiarra and come back home. Oceanfront Walk blondes are waiting to receive you."

"Not a chance. I need inner peace paired with high productivity. No woman can give me that. So, I'm good."

"Why do we need peace when there are beautiful women willing to spend the night in our beds?"

"I do. I need sanity."

"Right. That's why you called. Take my advice. Are Kiarra's legs straight and slender the way you prefer?"

"Nah. The woman has razor-sharp lips, generous boobs, butt and hips as round as the Rainbow Eucalyptus Trees along the sidewalk of *Sports Arena Boulevard*."

Laughing for the longest time, Jerrad came back after he caught his breath.

"Whoa! That's some hot boobs and butt combo. And she's revealing her true colours just like the trees. If you noticed, then you're interested in her. Say so."

"Are you kidding me? Haven't you listened to anything I've said? I'm not interested."

"I'm listening to what you haven't said, Ryder. If you weren't interested you wouldn't take notes."

"I'm done to talking to you about, Kiarra. Which celebrity boobs are you boosting with silicone now?"

"I don't augment and tell. How's the sales drive going on the other side?"

"Better than anticipated."

"Great work. Why you've got to do the work yourself is what beats me."

"My motive is deep rooted and you know it."

"Give Kiarra my regards when you hook up."

"Go clear your head. I want to have lunch."

"Yeah. Talk later."

Ryder pressed the end button and grimaced at his uneaten lunch.

Chapter 2 – Tough Luck

Kiarra

"How did you get my spare keys?" Ryder barked, getting to his feet, throwing on a grey V-neck, T-shirt over distressed dark jeans the second, Kiarra ushered herself into home uninvited.

Even though she showed up every week, his response was the same.

Kiarra kicked the front door shut.

A quick dart at his face revealed his vacant eyes had lit up despite his harsh tone. Although she was crazy to have obtained his spare key, in her defense, over the last four weeks or more, she had not seen Ryder bring home one grocery bag. Okay, so she kept tabs on his movements, so what? It was part of her tasks as his condo buddy to keep an eye out for him.

"What I expect, is for you to hurl these grocery bags out of my hands and on to the kitchen counter, so I'd feel lighter."

Glowering, he hurried to her side and grabbed the four big bags spread across her two hands and marched toward the kitchen island on the other end of the open-plan living room.

In the interim, she tried not to notice his butt and back muscles tense and flex. She also dismissed how her nipples hardened in her bra, under her mystic print over-sized chestnut T-shirt. Even the way her thighs tautened in her black denim jeans did not matter. That was not why she was in his condo.

Leaning over the dark wood island, he shoved the bags on to the black granite counter. The gold chain around his neck swayed along with his brusque rhythm. She preferred a guy who spotted a neck chain, any day. Not the thick, over-the-top rap singers' neck chain, or the type gangsters wore as part of their signature.

Ryder's was the stylish, thin gold jewellery that whispered, *drop a kiss around my neck*. Of course, she would never dream of dropping a kiss on his masculine ivory neck. Cuddling an elephant in the safari would have to happen first.

"Hey, be careful, big guy! There are eggs in there."

"That's the first thing you should have said," came his smart quip. A remark not followed by a *thank you*.

"Not everyone in the world is against you, Ryder. Ditch the boxing gloves."

"Go back to your condo, Kiarra. I'm not a charity case."

"Same song each week. With your overgrown beard dying for a shave, you look like a charity case," she scoffed, setting down her hand bag on one of the three white breakfast seats facing the kitchen island.

A muscle ticked along his neck.

Hmm. Someone was worked up and it was not her. Ryder's neck reminded her of a protective tower.

Resting one hand on the double-door dark-grey fridge-freezer, he fixed his ravishing hazel eyes on her.

"I don't follow," he grunted in a voice so deep it mimicked the roar of a lion.

"First of all, you need a shave," she insisted, waving at his face. "Second, maybe if you set aside your overly distressed, or should I say destroyed jeans and your irritating attitude, I'll take you seriously."

He crinkled his nose. "What? Are you my mom now? Telling me what to do, or wear in my own home?"

"Point of correction, not your own home. You pay rent, don't you?"

"Sorry to disappoint. I own this condo. That gives me the right to stop you from walking in here whenever you're bored."

Refusing to balk at his rancid mood, she unpacked one of the grocery bags. He stood there watching her like he had never seen a woman work with her hands.

"I don't need you shopping for me," he claimed when she was done unpacking the bag.

For some reason, she did not believe any word that came out of his mouth. It was not something she could explain. The man was miserable, clearly. That was the only thing he had to offer–misery. But she needed him know there was something better.

She turned away from him and opened the fridge door. A near-empty, cooling interior said *hi* to her.

"Why haven't you stocked up the fridge then?"

"Because I'm busy. And I don't need you to do it for me. Do you understand?"

Only a carton of beer and bottled water occupied the multiple refrigerator racks.

"So, you intend to drink yourself to death and have everyone in this building explain why no one took an interest in your well-being even though we saw you were on a mission to kill yourself?"

Folding his arms across his chest, he shook his head. "You must hate your life."

"As a matter of fact, I love my life."

"Really?" he sneered. "And you've got time in your lovely life to run after a guy who doesn't give a rat's ass about what you do for him?"

"It's for the greater good. You know the great saying, *love your neighbour as yourself.* If I were in your shoes, of course I'll never be so down and out. But if I were ever in your shoes, I'd hope someone would look my way and pick me up, even if I wasn't feeling grateful."

He balled his fingers into a tight fist and stamped it against the counter.

She blinked, but did not flinch.

"'I don't need you to 'pick me up', damn you!'" Ryder swore, his eyes a glinting green fire.

For a split second, she thought he would break something. Yet, she did not run away scared. Because beyond his macho exterior, she saw something in his eyes that begged her not to give up on him every week.

"Damn you, Ryder Blade!" she cussed back, something she rarely did. "Don't you ever cuss at me again. Do you hear me? I'm not some desperate brainless woman who needs your attention."

He bared his teeth. It was not a friendly grin, more like a ferocious warning.

"Using bullying tactic now?" She nudged his arm as she shuffled past. "Move. You don't scare me, big guy. Go find someone else to rattle with your dry rage."

Lifting his chin, he caught her arm with his left hand and peered down at her, his eyes thinned now.

"No one else crosses me like you do, Kiarra Wright. If I were you, I'd stay away. Stay far away from me."

Shaking her hand free, she turned her back on him. Of course, it was only because he did not hold her firmly, she let loose from his grip.

But her arm burned from his brief touch. Merry stars formed a queue from her forearm to her boobs.

"There's only one of me, Ryder Blade. You could never be me. I've got a heart."

She searched through the storage cupboards, got out frying pan, bowls and cooking utensils as if she had not just thrown a fat punch at his ego.

"What do you think you're doing?" he snarled.

"Go do whatever you do inside. When I'm done cooking, you can come out to eat, or you could unpack these two grocery bags."

Standing still, he squinted. Thin lines appeared at the corners of his eyes. He then raided her face with his gruelling gaze, dipped the pair to her cleavage and lingered there.

Goosebumps filtered to her skin.

Delightful shivers floated through her body.

Her nipples tingled with awareness.

She licked her lips and bowed her head, her fingers working of their own accord.

"This is my kitchen. Don't cook for me," he raved. "I don't take orders from you in my own home."

"Do your worst, Ryder. I'm not going anywhere."

When he did not physically throw her out after she called his bluff, or call 911, she realized he was all threat and nothing more. Ryder was like a dog that barked all day, stopping only after it was cuddled by the owner.

But she would never throw her arms around Ryder's neck, or kiss his sexy lips. Not in a million years would she thrust her boobs against his chiselled chest to feel his heat. Even stroking his nipples with her tongue was far-fetched. She would never hear him groan out her name in the throes of ecstasy after he had plunged what she imagined would be his hard length inside her wet heat. None of it will ever happen. That would be taking her rescue mission many steps too far.

"You're not listening," he sneered, wrenching her out of her sexual muse.

Startled, the utensils clanked as she knocked them against each other.

"Let's agree on one thing. If you stop ordering takeaway, I'll stop cooking for you."

"What happened to your boyfriend? You killed the poor guy with your needless attention and might I add, your overbearing attitude?"

"Mm-hmm. Why? Did you know the poor guy?"

She raised her eyes in time to see a flicker of interest whiz through his hazel eyes.

It was only then she grasped he had a sense of humour somewhere in his empty heart.

"What did you do with your evenings before I moved in here and became your pet project?" he breathed down her neck while she diced vegetables.

Laughing as she flipped over the two beef steaks on the pan shortly after, she eyeballed him.

"I was busy trying to write a book. Maybe I'll write about a new villain and kill him off half-way in."

He raised one eyebrow so high, his angled face twisted in a comical way, but his lips were scrubbed clean of any grin.

"As long as I'm not the villain."

"Um...I'm not so sure. Come to think of it. You're–"

"That's a joke, right? I bet you were lonely and sad before I moved in here."

"You would know, won't you? That's who you've become. *Lonely and sad.* What happened to turn you into this gloomy and resentful woman hater?"

For a moment, he stiffened and his eyes appeared vacant.

Cold chills poured into her spine in the interval.

"Ryder!" The guy got her more worried when he was quiet and looked lost in thought.

He blinked a couple of times, then he spun on his heel and marched toward the bedroom.

"Where are you going?" she heard herself ask against her will. "I'm making you dinner."

Moments later, she heard a door slam. That, was his reply. If the building was not built on some solid foundation, the whole structure would have crumbled. She was sure of it.

Exhaling, she stepped back from the stove. Shaking off the unsettling feeling in the pit of her stomach, she carried on cooking. He acted like a stroppy kid who had been denied his candy. When all he needed to say was, *oh, thank you, Kiarra for shopping for me. My fridge was empty. You're God sent.* The guy never heard such kind words in his life.

Honestly, she was confused about many things. About Ryder, yes. But the bigger muddle was related to herself. He made her feel things without even trying. The guy was a world-class jerk. A certified douchebag. Yet, acting like a jerk may be a sign he was hiding his deepest, insecure emotions.

With his narrowed gaze and warm breath, she had felt a fluttering in her stomach and a breathlessness that should only happen after kissing, or making out with someone she fancied on a profound level.

Cross with herself for getting carried away, she chewed on her bottom lip. While she cooked, the slushy feeling inside her grew heavier and sank to the pit of her belly with a thud. What a mess!

Get your head straightened, her conscience cried.

It would be pretty easy for anyone who looked from the outside to say, *Abandon Ryder. He doesn't deserve your attention.* But she just could not do it.

After she prepared rice and peas along with some potato salad and beef steak, she set a plate for Ryder. A large portion served on a square stone platter. Then she poured him a glass of water. After she folded a grey paper towel she bought from the store, she placed a cutlery set by the side of the plate.

She was out of her mind to serve him like a king when he was so undeserving of her culinary skills. But her actions reminded her of the sacrifice of someone special for the whole world. Her mom often quoted from the good book with her own added spin; *While we were still wallowing in our sins, Christ died for us, as undeserving as we are.*

Every time she wanted to pull the plug, to sit back in her condo and do nothing for Ryder, she got this bigger urge in her heart to check up on him. She worried something bad might happen to him and she would not forgive herself. It was the only reason she took his contemptible behaviour on the chin. Okay.

Maybe that was not the entire reason. But it was a huge part of it.

Two bags of grocery she brought in earlier still sat on the counter. Tough luck.

Instead of going after Ryder in his bedroom to coax him to eat however, she cleaned up the kitchen, grabbed her handbag and let herself out of his home.

Tonight, she needed to pamper herself.

Thursdays were full of meetings and visits to potential foster homes. So, it had been a pretty long day at work. Ryder had no idea the sacrifice she made by cooking him dinner.

Maybe one day, he might appreciate her effort.

Thirty minutes later, she soaked her tired body in her bath tub. Inhaling the sweet scent of lavender and fig in the bath crystals, she took a sip of Rosé wine from the glass and chewed on deep-fried southern-fried chicken. Seated in her steaming bath tub, she also feasted on biscuits and corn bread, the perfect accompaniments to crispy fried chicken. Of course, it would not be a homemade southern meal without biscuits.

She burped loud afterward.

Casually leaning her head against the bath tub rim, her thoughts drifted.

What is wrong with me? Nothing is wrong with me. I'm not ugly. I'm big, black and wonderful.

After her encounter with Ryder tonight, she had one more question for herself. *Am I as pathetic as Ryder alluded?*

No, her head insisted. *You're a good neighbour.*

"Ryder's the problem," she said out loud, binding her fingers along the border of the tub. "I hate that I keep showing up in his flat uninvited. It's been a month! Even the Lord knows, I should stay away from the guy's vile tongue."

But you give as good as you get, her conscience whispered.

Since Ryder moved into the condo building, she had become more homebound. She no longer frequented bars, restaurants and clubs with her colleagues and friends to have a great time.

That was confusing as hell.

"I'm not attracted to Ryder Blade," she told herself more than once like she needed to convince her brain.

Cocking her head, she tweaked her toes and grinned, whispering, "What if I'm attracted to him?"

Chapter 3 – You Happened

Ryder

Driving home from a business meeting took less than half-an-hour. But the drive dragged on forever as far as Ryder was concerned. Like he mentioned to Jerrad last week, he had signed a large number of clients and acquired new high net worth customers for the company. What started out as his field project had now increased the company client base and ultimately resulted in higher company earnings. The twin underlying goals had been achieved, not by waiting to read reports, but by a radical new approach.

Now parked in an empty parking lot spot, he made his way to *Cable Point Condos* building. Inside the elevator, his heart burped within his chest.

Tightening his fingers around his brief case handle, he ran his free hand through his hair before he stepped feet out of the elevator. To avoid running into any of the intrusive condo occupants, he now made it a habit to run up the less-used back staircase.

The moment Ryder unlocked his condo door, he stopped short.

The familiar sunshine scent mixed with fresh bouquet of flowers fragrance paraded up his nostrils. He lobbed in a gulp of air through his mouth. And exhaled through his nose. Kiarra was here.

A quick shudder spiked through his spine. The muscles in his abs flexed. Did she wait?

Frowning, he took quick strides through the hallway and landed in the open plan living and kitchen areas. Just as he suspected, or hoped, Kiarra Wright was seated on his couch with a book in one hand. When she saw him, a full smile exploded across her lips.

A soccer punch hit his gut. He swallowed. His chest widened as more air flooded inside. Was he happy to see her?

For one brief sec., he imagined a scenario where she was at home waiting for him to come back from work. As quickly as it came, the flash disappeared like a mirage and he cleared his throat. Flames whipped past his groin. His big boy stiffened in his pants.

Although, there was nothing sultry about her glance from across the room, yet his pulse raced. His breathing quickened. It was a weird feeling. Kiarra was one woman who needed to stay out of his horny radar for many reasons. He must not imagine his hands juggling her boobs, or his tongue tracking her nipples until they tightened with an ache so deep, she begged him to suck her. Even sliding his tongue along her cleavage down to her hot heat to taste her fruity extracts was an impossible thought. And so was the reality of ever thrusting his aching erection inside her wet heat.

He groaned as the lockdown between his legs sharpened.

"Should I ask what you're doing here on a Friday evening?"

Jerk! That was the last thing he wanted to ask. Raising one hand in the air, he retracted his question. "Ignore that. Hey, did you have a great day?"

His heart hit his chest hard while he waited for her response. Would she bite off his head?

After a heartbeat, she propped one elbow on the arm of the couch and pressed her cheeks on her palm.

"Yeah. And you?"

"Mm-hmm."

Stunning! Her eyes, the exact colour of roasted, ground coffee beans fixed on his own. Then he noted her skin was as smooth as a velvet leaf in summer. Her dark, glistening curls bounced around her ears and loop earrings as she angled her head. He wanted to tuck the stray tresses behind her earlobes and whisper something wild in her ear, so she could laugh for him and, with him.

"Are you okay?" Kiarra asked.

A look of concern marred her rounded jaw and delicately carved cheekbones.

Straddling one dining chair he grabbed within reach, he set down his brief case.

"What do you want from me, Kiarra Wright?"

"Nothing."

"I'm not shocked you're here. Which is ridiculous because you should've better things to do with your Friday evening, especially when you look the way you do in that black dress."

Setting her book aside, she slanted her head and grinned.

"What's wrong with my dress?"

"You want me to say it? Fine. It's gorgeous!"

Wide-eyed she bent her head and gave her sequined art deco cocktail dress a glance over.

Sharpening his gaze, he took the opportunity to dance around her full curves made prominent in the knee-length dress. What happened to the over-sized t-shirts and jeans pants she favoured? The dress emphasized her curvy cleavage and hips that had no hiding place on the couch. *Attractive!*

His breathing turned shallow.

"Um. I'm surprised I'm here, trust me. I've got better things to do. I got invited to a party and my friends are out clubbing. But I knew you'd end up on your own, so I thought I'd check on you."

He shrugged, and ran one hand through his hair.

"I'm good. Work was good. Everything is great," he stressed his words.

"So, you're not new in San Diego?"

Her eyes filled with curiosity. He noticed her long, dark lashes fluttered back and forth. Wait. Did she wear false lashes? These seemed long and beautiful.

Again, his pulse flirted up and down.

"Ryder?"

"N-no," he fluffed, nodding.

"Aha! I thought so."

"What does that mean?"

"You know, you go and come like a local. It got us thinking. Where did you stay before you moved here?"

Straight-faced, he shrugged. "That I can't say."

"Why? You work for law enforcement?"

"That would be a no."

"If you make this any more difficult than it is, you'll be on this interrogating chair for a while."

An amazing smile shot up her face. Stars twirled in her deep brown eyes and the pair glowed like the moon on a cold, dark night.

Shaking off the warm sensations winding inside his chest, he declared. "I didn't realize I was confined to the seat I pulled up myself."

She grinned. "Now you're confined until I say you're not. Got it?"

"What can I do for you, Kiarra?"

"Answer a few quick questions and I'll let you get a drink, then you'll come back and we'll continue."

For many minutes, a fancy buzz floundered inside his belly. All his life, he had never met a woman who called his bluff and put him in his place. He had raged at her. Cussed her. Was outright rude when all she did was be good to him, and she had stayed. Kiarra did not only hang around, she raged at him in her own way. Before today, she had given him many chances to redeem himself. And she was generous in a special way that was rare. Yet, he had pissed over her face. The least he could do now was to give in to her small demand.

"OK. Go ahead," he confirmed.

She gasped and blinked.

"What? You're not going to cuss, or rant? What happened to put you in a good mood, Ryder Blade?"

"You happened!"

He promptly shut his mouth. Those two words should not have hopped out of his lips.

The woman seated on the couch crinkled her eyes and nose.

"'Explain. What do you mean by 'you happened'?'"

"There's nothing to explain. I met you here and–"

"And what? I put you in a good mood?" she chopped off the rest of his statement and supplied the ending.

Throwing her head back on the couch, she laughed.

"I'm in shock. That's a big lie and we both know it."

He sighed in relief. She did not believe his words. That was a lucky escape. All he had to do going forward was to think before he said anything.

"What's your question, Kiarra?"

"Ah, yeah. Do you have friends? One? Never seen anyone drop in to say hi."

"I've got a friend who's closer than a brother. He's great. Believe me, your concern is misplaced. Next question?"

"What's his name?"

"Jerrad Stone."

"How long have you been friends?"

His conversation with Jerrad the last time they spoke provided the motivation to explain further.

"Since preschool," he told her, his thoughts in chaos.

Shaking her head, she blew out her cheeks.

"That's hard to believe. I'm sorry."

He raised both eyebrows. "Excuse me?"

"I don't believe you have a friend."

"Because he doesn't come around like you do?"

"There's a reason he's staying away. For someone you've known since preschool I would've thought he would care enough to check in on you."

"What planet do you live on? Jerrad's got a life." Of course, that life included hooking up with different women most nights. But he would not divulge that bit of information. "I'm not a kid."

"What does Jerrad do?"

"Plastic surgeon."

"Are you sure?" Giving him a sceptical glance, she grinned harder.

He suppressed the grin warming his jaw.

"Now what? You think I'm making it up?"

Eyes rolling upward, she nodded. "Sums it up."

Needled by her taunts, he got out his cell phone and pressed Jerrad's number.

Fine lines creased her brow as she murmured.

"Leave it on speaker. I want to hear you chatting with your imaginary friend."

Stroking his groomed beard, he waited for Jerrad to answer. It rang seven times. Jerrad was probably out partying already. When he did not answer on the eighth ring, he shrugged.

"He's probably busy."

"Well, try again," Kiarra insisted, frying him with her punishing, heated gaze.

A short pause stretched between them while he frisked her with his eyes in return. Dark arched brows pulled inward as her scrutiny intensified. Her long nose tapered into a round tip and flared in a cute way. Cupid bow shaped lips, now lined featured a pale pink gloss which served to pull his gaze and muddle his thoughts each time she opened her mouth. He imagined her graceful lips softened against his as he dragged in deep breaths.

His erection thickened, nudging between his legs.

Awareness heightened for long minutes as the silence solidified. And as she turned toward the window, there was this movement on top of her cheekbone. He thought it was a speck, but it was not— just the easy-going April fading light swiftly bouncing off her brown skin giving it a golden lustre.

"Go on," she whispered under her breath without blinking.

He blew out air from his nose as he did what she wanted. For the life of him, he could not understand why he allowed her to take the lead. This was his turf. Ryder Blade had never taken orders from any woman in any relationship.

However, to salvage his reputation, and as proof he was not lying, he hoped, Jerrad would dig out his head from romping with his latest blonde to pick his call. This was important. Kiarra's eyes did not leave his face. And he heard his pulse wrestle for control.

Before he could press J's number again, his cell phone pinged, indicating an incoming call. It was J. With his eyes back on the same level as Kiarra's, he answered the call.

"Bro, what's up? I missed your call," J said. "You're not dying, are you?" As usual, his response was direct and sandwiched with humour.

Ryder chuckled. "Not tonight, I'm not."

Kiarra giggled, covering her mouth with one hand to muffle the sound.

"Someone wants to confirm if we're friends," he told J. "That's all. Get off the line once you do that."

Inside his chest, the bar of excitement was at its peak. He penned it down to anticipation.

"Someone doubts our brotherly love for each other? Who's that? As long as long as it's not your crazy neighbour–"

"Shut up, idiot!" Ryder interrupted.

Jerrad's description of Kiarra stabbed his heart.

Tucking in her chin, Kiarra gave a close-lipped smile before she spoke.

"Yeah. It's me, his crazy neighbour, Kiarra Wright. Did he tell you I make sure he eats homemade food instead of ruining his muscles with fast food and dying on everyone, huh? Did he also tell you I keep him company, so he doesn't die of loneliness, lose his ungrateful mind and jump off the cliff in one of his gloomy moods?"

Wincing inside at her harsh outburst, Ryder averted his gaze. He deserved her rant. Kiarra had done nothing more than to look out for him and he had bad mouthed her the first chance he got. Well, he had no idea she was a generous woman with a good heart who wanted nothing from him.

"Oh, Ryder told me every detail and you're right. He sounded ungrateful to me. Forgive him for my sake."

Kiarra chuckled. Jerrad joined in and his laughter rushed out of the phone unfiltered. Relieved, she was not mad at him, Ryder rubbed his nose with his forefinger. He and Jerrad dodged Kiarra's bullet.

"How are you doing, Jerrad Stone?" Kiarra resumed speaking. "Ryder's been telling you a bunch of crap about me. Well, now we've met officially."

"Wow! Hey Kiarra. My hands are clean. Great to meet you too. I spoke out of turn at the start. Can you let it slide?"

"I already did. I won't be having this chat if I didn't. Anyway, I wanted to know if Ryder had a friend."

"Yeah. We go back a long way. We're brothers from different moms. You feel me?"

"I get that now," she quipped, skewing her head, accidentally appearing sexier as her curls grazed the side of her face and, shoulders bared in her sleeveless dress. "Thanks for the confirmation."

"You said earlier, Ryder's unhappy over there."

"Yeah. Ryder's lonely and grumpy most of the time," Kiarra clarified as if he needed a host of intervention to straighten his life.

Ryder cleared his throat and waved one hand in the air. "Enough, you two. Friendship over."

"Nice talking to you, Kiarra. Thank you for keeping an eye on my brother. I owe you."

"You owe me nothing, Jerrad. Keep in touch with Ryder. We don't want him to do something stupid."

"You think he's suicidal?" J pushed, angling for a diagnosis he could hold on to for their future banter.

Jerrad was enjoying the conversation far more than Ryder wanted. It was the same with Kiarra, as her face became animated as she chatted.

"Never met two crazy people in my life! Get off my phone, J! Go do what you do best."

Jerrad and Kiarra laughed.

"Missing you, bro," Jerrad added, still chuckling. "Have fun you two. I'm going back to my business."

"Liar! Say hi to whoever she is," Ryder countered.

"Yeah, right."

He ended the call before Jerrad said too much.

"Who's your best friend?" he asked the stunning woman seated on his couch the moment, J was off air.

"Mine?" She tapped her fingers on her cleavage.

Low voltage electricity coursed through his groin. He jerked on his seat. Gripping the chair with one hand, he undid his top buttons for air to cool down his arousal.

"That's what I asked, Kiarra."

"Taleisha. Her name's Taleisha Hill. She's been my friend for a long time."

"You've been friends for how long?"

"Since college."

"Great. How long have you been in San Diego?" Suddenly, it occurred to him he knew next to nothing about the woman who had sacrificed her time and money to keep him sane in every sense of the word.

"Nah!" She swiped her finger in the air, pairing it with a shake of her head. "You've not earned the privilege of asking me personal questions when you hug your profile to your chest."

Her eyes descended to his chest as she ended the statement. Up in a flash, her eyes nailed his again.

Dampness spread across his chest as his heart jolted in his chest. He swallowed to work out the heat flushing his body.

"Remember, I do the asking, Ryder."

He raised his brows and slowly eased out of the hot chair. "I need a drink."

She pressed her lips together before taunting him.

"That's a getaway excuse if I ever heard one. Get some water to drink. I'm not going anywhere soon. It's Friday evening."

Chuckling inside, he lunged to his feet and headed toward his bedroom.

"You skipped the kitchen stop. Isn't that where the drinks are, hm?"

"Got a fridge in my bedroom."

He shrugged off his jacket as he moved farther away from her. His breathing came out shallow.

Kiarra exchanged the kind of banter that made him feel great. She teased him in a way no woman had done. Before he turned the corner to his room, he hesitated and did a full spin to face her.

"What do I do to earn the privilege?"

Instead of meeting his gaze and giving him an answer, she looked down and stared at the pages of her book. Her lashes swept over her eyes screening what he wanted to see.

Then she muttered, "Don't know what you mean."

"Yes, you do. Tell me."

"Go, get your drink. Why do you want to know anything about your crazy neighbour?"

"Forget I asked."

"You owe me an apology, Ryder. Even then you still won't have any rights. Do you hear me?"

"Suit yourself."

"Is that an apology?"

"Give me a break."

"Go to hell!"

Irked because she did not let his nasty comment to Jerrad slide, he entered his bedroom and shut the door. Or to be precise, he slammed the door.

Chapter 4 – Lost My Mind

Kiarra

Sitting with her friend in the café a week later, Kiarra glowered at her drink as if it was poisonous.

"Girl, spill. What's eating you up?" Taleisha Hill, her friend from junior high asked with a short laugh.

"Is it that obvious?" Kiarra groaned.

"You've not touched your southern fried chicken. That's a first."

Taleisha threw a handful of fries in her mouth before she took a bite from her hamburger.

Idly, Kiarra dipped fries in ketchup and a small piece of chicken in hickory barbecue sauce, but set it down. "Look, it's one of my neighbours."

Taleisha wiped her stained lips with a paper napkin. "Which one?"

Sighing, Kiarra waved one hand. "He's new. You've not met him."

Taleisha ate all her fries after dipping them into mayo. "What's his name?"

"Ryder Blade."

Twisting her lips here and there, Taleisha sipped from her drink and then swallowed.

"I'll be wary of any guy with that name, seriously?"

Absently, Kiarra started to eat her fries one after the other. "Why is that?"

"For one, that name's shady. Anyway, what did he do to get you all tangled up like this?"

Around them, the servers bustled around, wiped unoccupied tables and cleaned the floor. Kiarra did not notice. Even the black and white geometric café wall decor she often gushed about went unnoticed.

"That's the annoying thing. He's done nothing except tell me in harsh, clear words and tone to get out of his life and stay away."

"Whoa!" Taleisha's eyes bulged. "Excuse me? And what did you say to him? I hope you put him where he belongs, in the trash?"

Kiarra let out a long sigh. "That's the other thing. I got his spare key, so I let myself into his condo weekly to check on him because I get worried about him."

Laughing and shaking her head, Taleisha spilled her drink. Steadying her cup, her friend wiped the mess and confronted her with a questioning gaze.

"Spare key? Worried about your new neighbour? Okay there's more to this story? What am I missing?"

Kiarra massaged her brow with her fingers. There was no simple way to explain her awkward situation.

"When Ryder first moved in–" she started to explain. "–the guys assigned me to keep a close eye on him, you know, to let him know how we do things–"

"The usual break in party, the condo buddy thing," Taleisha supplied.

"Exactly. Except that, Ryder wasn't interested, or friendly. Then I saw he hadn't even unpacked all of his belongings after two weeks. He's always gloomy and aggrieved, but I feel there's more to him. And I know he must be lonely and in need of company."

"You sound like you've fallen for this guy." Taleisha snapped her fingers. "Kiarra wake up! The slumber party is over."

Kiarra swallowed the small bite of hamburger in a rush and sipped from her soda.

"Are you nuts? Of course, I've not fallen for him."

"Oh! Then you're seriously infatuated with this bad guy. Is that it? I need an explanation that makes sense. How's his gloomy mood your problem? And so, what if he decides to live from his unpacked boxes?"

"'I'm not 'infatuated'. Just a little attracted to him. And it's only a little.'"

Taleisha laughed, and tapped her friend's hand.

"I knew it! That's the first thing you've said all evening that makes any sense. Now describe him."

Giggling, Kiarra shut her eyes. "He's really tall, like six three, or four, or five." She opened her eyes.

"Skinny, fat? What does he look like?"

"Not at all. He's a solid block of delicious muscle, sculpted by the best hands. Tattoos sweep across his arms and chest like a whirlwind. Fascinating hazel eyes are like magnets. His skin colour is a nice ivory shade, and when he's pissed, his colour comes alive in a gorgeous pink hue. I grocery shop and cook for him because his fridge is usually empty."

"Stop right there!" her friend ordered. "Cook for him? Shop? What's going on with you and Ryder?"

Kiarra shrugged. "Nothing. I cook and check up on him and he acts like a jerk and tells me to get lost. I think he resents women in general. He wasn't pleasant to anyone at our last barbecue party."

"You've either lost your mind, or he's cast a spell on you. Which is it?"

With her shoulders slumped now, Kiarra groaned. "That's why I needed to talk to you. I've lost my mind for sure. It's no longer a secret."

"Lord have mercy! OK. One, stop visiting without an invitation. Two, quit shopping. Three, stop cooking for him, Kiarra! You've never cooked for any guy before. Don't start now. He hasn't earned it."

"I know that. But he won't eat healthy otherwise."

"Look around you. Do you go about feeding every unhealthy-eating American on the streets, or in this café? Ryder Blade's not your responsibility."

Rolling her eyes upward, Kiarra buried her face in her hands.

"Come over sometime. I want you to meet, Ryder first. He's got this commanding presence. You'll go a mile for him without his say so. It's weird."

"There's no way I'm doing anything for a man who as cold-hearted as you've described. What does he do for a living?" Taleisha feasted on the chicken.

"I've got no clue."

"Have you asked him?"

"Along with a thousand other questions he never answers."

"Go back a step. How often do you go to his condo?"

"Say once to twice a week."

"That's crazy! Where does Zack fit in all this?"

"Zack's deal is the way it's been for the two years, or more. Nothing has changed."

"Okay. Here's what I'm going to do. I'll stop by your office on the days you've got an urge to check up on, Ryder. We'll have a nice time instead."

"Then what?" asked Kiarra with a confused grin.

"We'll go on a girls' night out. You and me. Maybe we'll attract the men that deserve us."

Kiarra shrugged, and leaned back in her seat. "Um-hmm. Sounds like a plan," she muttered.

"Why aren't you excited?"

"I'll be when it actually happens."

"One time, Kiarra! It was only one time I didn't show. Now you sound as if it's my bad habit."

The two women giggled.

"Told you I'll never let you forget it happened. Has your workaholic boss being transferred yet?"

Taleisha worked as an Account Executive at a reputable accounting firm. But her working hours stretched till whenever her boss left the office.

"Not yet. He lets me leave on time now."

"Why? He grew a conscience?"

"Um-hmm. Maybe."

"What's does that really mean?" Kiarra sniggered, pointing at her friend's giggling face. "I see the sparkle in your dark eyes, girl. You're falling for your boss?"

"No! I'm falling for my boss's boss."

"Oh Lord! Girl, you've aimed higher. Wait, isn't Evan Truman married?"

"Recently divorced," Taleisha corrected, winking.

"Ugh!"

"What? The guy is free!"

"More damaged than free."

"More damaged than Ryder Blade?"

The two women threw back their heads as they laughed at their precarious relationships.

"The heart wants what the heart wants," said Kiarra snickering. "Where are the good guys? Free. Loving. Compassionate-and-ready to-marry types?"

"They're all in the romance novels on my E-reader," countered, Taleisha turning up her nose.

Kiarra wiped the corner of her eyes after another laughing sprout. This was why friends were the best. A good dose of after-work laughter to dispel the gloomy thoughts of Ryder Blade.

Yes, Ryder wanted nothing to do with her. That much was clear. He despised her presence, yet she could not get him out of her thoughts. Not even when she was out with her bestie. He dominated her private moments. Yet, she did not resent him for any of it.

"What are you going to do about your tangled emotions, Kiarra?"

"Nothing I guess."

"On the other hand, you could throw caution to the wind and make a move first."

"I already did. He shut me down."

"Never give up, girl. Better to try and fail, hmm?"

"Ryder's one mountain I don't wish to climb."

"Then we'll find replacements," Taleisha suggested.

"Yeah!"

What was it about Ryder that made Kiarra want to save him from himself? Was it his enthralling hazel eyes that made her tremble inside? Or, was it his bad boy personality? Maybe it had more to do with the fact his entire physique was like an icy muscular fountain waiting for her to lick him until he shuddered with red-hot passion. Whatever it was, it was turning her into a crazy version of herself. That was not a good thing.

Ryder Blade was nothing like her previous exes, so what was the attraction? If she could answer the lingering question, she could get rid of her obsession.

Chapter 5 – No Big Deal

Ryder

Waking up to find a pair of alabaster supple legs strewn across his own, Ryder rubbed his eyes with the pad of his fingers.

His eyes burned from lack of sleep.

His head pounded from drinking too many shots.

What the hell?

Then, he heard the clinking of keys in the distance.

That woman was here! Kiarra. His nightmare neighbour! The one that whizzed into his condo at any time as if she co-owned the place. Yet, he could not bring himself to physically throw her out. It was not because he could not do it. He had thought about it a number of times. There was something pure about her. She was dignified despite his crappy attitude.

Muttering insane expletives, he shrugged off Hailey's legs from his body and sat up. His heart pumped in a rush. Was it from excitement, or dread? Before he could pinpoint which one it was, his intrusive neighbour waltzed inside his bedroom.

Damn!

"What the hell are you doing in here?" he whispered, hoping not to wake up his guest.

Ignoring him completely after giving him a nasty glare, Kiarra marched to the window, pulled a fistful of heavy grey curtains and yanked them apart.

Early summer rays basted the glass and streamed in through the window panes, splashing glorious light across his bedroom. Too harsh for his sleep-deprived eyes, he shielded his face with the palm of one hand.

"Wake up, sluggard!" Kiarra announced in her confident voice. "It's a bright new day filled with new hopes and possibilities."

"Get out, Kiarra!" he blustered. She had no right to come in here.

Beside him, Hailey woke up, startled. Rubbing her face, she mumbled, "What's going on?"

"Time to go, lady. He's done with you," Kiarra declared as if she was his mouthpiece.

Standing with hands akimbo, her roasted coffee eyes sparked with fiery heat. Her tone brooked no argument. Another over-sized t-shirt paired with white denim along with her dark curls tumbling out of the messy bun on her head gave her this image of having just rolled out of bed. Kiarra reeked of sex appeal. He shook his head to dispel the notion.

"And who are you?" Hailey muttered, getting to her feet in a sluggish haze.

"I'm his concerned cousin," Kiarra snapped.

"She's my intrusive neighbour," he responded at the same time as Kiarra. He shook his head.

Clothed in just her red bra and panties, Hailey stretched, yawned and reached for her mini skirt and snug top, pulling them on slowly.

"Oh! Decide, Ryder. Is she your cousin, or your neighbour?" Hailey glanced at the wall clock.

"I'm his cousin and neighbour. Goodbye," Kiarra replied jutting out her chin. "Go home. Hurry."

He almost chuckled at Kiarra's aggressive posture. To avoid her condemning gaze however, he faced Hailey. "We'll talk. Later."

"He won't be needing your services again," Kiarra added with a sneer like she was his girlfriend.

Definite warm sensations plagued his body at the thought. His pulse and breathing even quickened.

"It was a booty call, not a paid service," Hailey clarified, pushing her feet into her pair of black ankle boots. "I thought he asked you to get out, Kiarra."

"Ryder? I need you in the kitchen." Kiarra said, her tone terse. She ignored Hailey's direct question.

He had never seen Kiarra in this mood. For that reason, he felt guilty, like she had caught him doing something wrong to her. But he had not. They were not dating. But she had visited every week for the last eleven weeks. Maybe she had earned some right.

Jumping to his feet, he pulled down the hem of his cotton stretch boxers. "To do what? It's Saturday."

Kiarra averted her gaze as he adjusted his boxers.

"See you, Ryder. Sort out your neighbour," Hailey said out loud. She kissed his cheek before swinging out of his bedroom. "Bye, Kiarra. Until next time."

"There won't be a next time," Kiarra maintained.

"Why did you storm into my bedroom?" he barked once Hailey shut the door. "It's my private area."

Though he stood in his underpants, he did not rush to throw on some clothes.

"Because I can." She angled her head. "Deal with it. I hope you used a condom? STDs are not for aliens."

"My sex life is none of your business. You've got no right to barge into my bedroom and kick out my guest. Hailey's my–"

"'Guest?'" she scoffed. "Or booty call?" Somehow the words sounded like cuss words the way she said it.

"It's my life. I do what I want. Do I know how many guys you've invited to your condo? Let's talk numbers. How many guys?"

She shrugged. "Pancakes. Come and make us pancakes with blueberries for breakfast."

The whole time, she did not stare at his face, or body directly. That hurt. Like she thought he was dirty and did not deserve her stunning gaze. Shocked by her demand however, his jaw dropped. When he recovered, he queried.

"Excuse me? Who says I'm making pancakes?"

She whisked her face around to scowl at him.

"Me. Put on some clothes and join me in your spotless kitchen. It's crying for attention."

He blinked. "So, my kitchen cried to you and now you want me to make pancakes for you?"

Smiling, she nodded. "Mm-hmm."

Jitters surged up and down inside his abs where her eyes trailed. And his groin got a strong vibe.

"That about sums it up," Kiarra asserted. "I'll be in the kitchen. Hurry up. I've not got all day."

After she sashayed out of his bedroom, he hurried to the bathroom, brushed his teeth and had a brisk shower. There was no way he would show up in Kiarra's presence smelling like yesterday's flowers.

The entire bedroom still smelled of her sensual fresh floral scent–a combination of heady patchouli, jasmine and rose.

When he stepped out to the living room about fifteen minutes later, he saw Kiarra seated on one of the breakfast seats in the kitchen.

She was flipping through his *Men's Health* magazine—a recent purchase by the way. Her scent extended an invitation to him just like a soft blanket did on a cold winter night.

Patting his groomed beard, he pulled in air through his nose and thrust his hands inside the pockets of his cuffed navy jogging bottom.

"At last! I hope you smell better, Ryder."

"Make the pancakes yourself, Kiarra."

Twisting her neck to give him a side glance, she gestured with her right hand.

"The fun stuff is here. Come over."

It seemed her rage was gone. What a relief. Something about her stopped him from throwing her out of his condo and his life. Courage. Maybe it was her extra confidence that cut him to size. Just might be what he admired. Her tenacity too. Her stubborn will to get him out of his rut, no matter what. Only someone who cared deeply would put up with his trash. He knew it. Now she had advanced to ordering him around—something he hated.

"I don't cook." He crossed his arms across his chest.

"Then, you'll learn." Creasing her nose, she waved aside his remark. "OK. Someone smells like a billion dollars."

"And why will I learn?"

His ego got a huge boost from her compliment.

"Because it's a life skill you need to survive."

"Says who? I can order pancakes with any topping and flavour I want."

"Wrong," she insisted, slipping down from the chair. "Today, you'll do something different. It probably terrifies you to cook, but trust me, you won't die trying. You'll survive and love it."

"You don't know what I'll love. Stop sounding like a mom."

Lifting her soft-angled brows, she asked. "Do I? If I sound like my mom, that'll be cool. Meanwhile, stand here." She pointed to the shopping bags on the table. "Empty the bags. Everything you need to make American pancakes is in there."

"My mom tried to teach me, I declined."

Kiarra had gone shopping again? He had never thanked her, or repaid her in anyway. His conscience troubled him to great length. He moved over to stand near her.

"Why are you doing this, Kiarra?"

"Hey, I'm not your mom. I'll not take no for an answer. So, Ryder Blade, take out the flour, milk, eggs and everything else and get on with it."

Just like that. His whole body lit up with a fire he had not experienced in a very long time. His lips widened into a grin. And he stared at his neighbour. She rested her head on her hands and her eyes laughed with him.

Warmth coursed through his body and constricted his chest. He licked his lips and did what she wanted. After he unpacked the bags, he lifted his head. It felt great to satisfy her, even in a small way.

"Thank you for shopping, Kiarra."

"For this one, or the many times I've shopped?"

Turning away, he opened the storage cupboards and got out the pan and utensils he hoped he needed.

"What happened to you overnight? Did having sex with, Hailey make you appreciate the simpler things in life? I've been trying to reform you for 3months."

"For everything." She was needling him to speak about Hailey, but he had no intention of doing that.

"OK. You're going to prepare fluffy American pancakes with blueberries and cinnamon."

"Eggs, milk, sugar, flour, baking powder. Is that it?"

He liked the easy way conversation flowed between them despite the Hailey situation.

"Yeah. Those are the basic ingredients. Do you like cinnamon?"

He nodded. "Of course. Which American doesn't?"

"And blueberries?"

"All the time. My mom made me pancakes with blueberries and cinnamon most days."

Kiarra stared at him. "Till you got to high school?"

Sure, he could mimic what he saw his mom do countless times, he knocked one egg against the rim of the glass bowl. The egg spilled on the counter top before he could pry it apart and direct it into the bowl.

"No big deal," Kiarra said, plucking a fist full of tissues and handing them to him across the counter.

"Wipe the spill and try again. This time, crack the centre of the egg shell with a fork. Then set the fork down, use your God-given two hands to fully split the egg and empty the content into the bowl."

"Why didn't you mock me?"

"That won't make any sense. You said you'd never cooked before. So, I don't expect you to know what you're doing. But I'll give you brownie points for effort."

"My mom knocked it against the bowl every time."

Kiarra took an egg and cracked it against the rim of the bowl, the exact way his mom did it and she emptied it into the bowl.

"Like so?" She winked. "That's the how the culinary experts do it."

An uneasy jolt sliced through his gut, so he swallowed the lump in his throat. But his heart boomed in his chest. He knew, Kiarra was not the flirty type. Then why was she winking?

"Carry on," she encouraged with a lovely grin.

"My mom did it the exact way. It's weird."

He shrugged and cracked the eggs with a fork instead. It was an easier technique.

Kiarra shrugged. "Tell me about your mom."

Instead of speaking, he followed the recipe she printed out on the counter top and made ten round pancakes with blueberries and cinnamon.

"I'm very proud of my pancakes."

"See? It feels good to make an edible meal."

After the two of them sat down to eat at the breakfast table, he nudged her elbow.

"Pass the maple syrup, Kiarra."

She drizzled a bit across her four pancakes.

"Use the P word," she told him, raising her brows.

"Please."

Only then did she hand over the syrup.

"My mom's a neurosurgeon," he finally opened up.

Kiarra coughed a little.

He spared her a quick glimpse. "You're not dying, are you?"

"No." she coughed again.

So, he pushed one bottled water her way and brewed her fresh coffee with a dash of milk and sugar.

"Thank you," Kiarra muttered after she had some water and a sip of coffee. "That's some great tasting coffee. What brand is that?"

"*Rich Earth Coffee.* Haven't you had it before?"

"No way. I would've remembered. Where do you buy that?"

"In the grocery stores. Haven't you been to *Swami's Café Point Loma* two streets away? They serve it."

"Never stopped there. Always *Starbucks*, or *Local Krave.*"

"About time you tried something authentic."

"Will do." She took another sip and shut her eyes. "Why haven't you made this for me before?"

Good question. He shrugged. "Don't know. Didn't think." *Because you're a douche bag*, his heart blared.

"Too busy being a jerk," Kiarra concluded, and she was not far from the truth.

"Maybe."

He woofed down his meal. The fluffy pancakes tasted better than his mom's. Sweet success rushed through his head. It felt good to finally win.

"You were saying your mom's a neurosurgeon? That's an accomplishment. What's her name?"

"Lindsay. Pancake was the only food she made when I was growing up."

"Why? She was too busy to cook?"

"Something like that." He strived for a casual tone. Then, he carried his plate and cutlery to the sink.

"Growing up, it must've been cool to have a smart mom, Ryder."

"'Depends on what 'cool' meant to you. To me, it meant she never made it to PTA, fundraising events, any school rendition, or games. Being called the kid without a mom wasn't cool.'"

Looking up from her empty plate, Kiarra nodded.

"Too busy saving others. I get it. Please don't tell me you've still got abandonment issues?"

"Do they really go away?"

Shaking her head, she sighed. "White kids. Always blowing feelings out of proportion. Your mom was busy doing amazing work, where was your dad?"

"I don't appreciate you ranking me with every other white kid you know." All of a sudden, he wanted her to see him as different. Maybe even special.

"I wasn't."

"We're all shaped by our upbringing, one way, or another. Mine happens to be the way it is, right?"

"Not always. Yes, sometimes."

He rounded on her. "You sound confused. Do you think I've got abandonment issues?"

"That's not my call to make. I don't know you well enough to make such a conclusion."

"True. You don't know me at all. So, stop making snide remarks. Not cool." She irked him quickly, but he was more pissed at himself.

"Wow! Don't jump down my throat, Ryder. We're having a chat and I'm trying to get to know you."

"You can be very annoying."

In his mind, he was more worked up about the fact she did not think he was special. Why did that matter?

"I apologize. Your pancakes taste great by the way. For a first time cook, you killed it."

A slow grin warmed his face. And his anger dissipated instantly. It meant a lot to him to get an approval rating from his dignified neighbour.

"Thank you," he whispered.

"My pleasure. No one is too old to learn."

Narrowing his eyes, he asked. "How old are you?"

"Thirty-one. What about you?"

"Much younger than you." He turned around and rinsed his plate.

"You wish!" She made a clicking sound with her teeth. "If you're younger than me I'll throw myself out of the window."

Wild laughter erupted from his mouth. He laughed so much he knocked the dish against the faucet. It cracked, scattering into large pieces in the sink.

As Kiarra giggled, she also hit her elbow against the counter edge. "Ouch!" she squeaked.

When he was done laughing, he picked up the broken pieces and shoved them in the trash can.

"I'll wash my plate myself," she said. "I can't trust you not to break this one."

Grinning, he stepped away from the sink.

"It's the first time we've laughed together in this condo. I broke a dish and you knocked your elbow. That's something to remember, Kiarra."

"Mm-hmm. Let's not forget why we laughed. You claimed to be under thirty-one. Are you a politician?"

"Of course not. You wish I was older than you?"

She washed and rinsed the plate, mugs and cutleries. "I'll say you're thirty-seven at least."

Grunting, he rubbed his hair to point at the centre.

"Do I look that old to you?"

Every time she cooked, Kiarra washed up the cooking utensils and dinnerware. She also wiped down the counter.

The women he slept with never offered to do grocery shopping, or clean his kitchen. They never offered to cook, simple. But they were always ready to order whatever they wanted to eat. In fact, he also thought it was the best option until he met his neighbour from a different background. Kiarra made him remember home. In many ways, each time she glided into his condo her presence and actions filled him with nostalgia.

"Ryder, if I were completely honest, I'd say you look much older."

Laughing again, he covered his face with both hands. "That's right! I look sixty. And you're fifty-six."

Laughter whipped out of her mouth as she rocked against the sink. She doubled over the counter top and threw him an, I'm-going-to-kill-you gaze.

"Where are the wrinkles around my eyes and brows, hmm?" she accused, wearing a mock grin.

"Does it hurt now? Do I have wrinkles?"

"Mm-hmm. Many gloomy wrinkles around your eyes. Your prominent jawline and square forehead would've been gorgeous otherwise."

"Really? Okay. You've got judges' wrinkles around your otherwise beautiful coffee-brown eyes."

"OK. One thing is clear. You think my eyes are beautiful and I think yours are gorgeous."

"Never said that," he denied, yet his heart agreed.

"Oh yes you did. I heard it. Can't take it back now, Ryder. Where was your dad while your mama was doing some good? Let's get back to our previous talk."

Giving Kiarra compliments would probably make her feel big-headed. She was already very confident.

"My dad was a car salesman. Never around."

"Oh. Any brothers, or sisters?"

"One sister. Alana's older."

"Is Alana married?"

"Yeah. To Alex. No kids yet if that's your next question. They've been trying for a while."

"It wasn't, but good to know. Now you're in a rare talking mood, let me ask. Have they tried adopting?"

Their easy back and forth chat happened across the kitchen counter like they were close friends.

"Are you a lawyer?" was his quick reply.

"No. Why?"

"Why are you so interested in me?"

"Because you're my neighbour."

"And you know everyone else in the other condos just as well? You've got their spare keys and you intrude whenever you want?"

Kiarra stiffened. An interval followed. Then she wiped her hand, grabbed her bag and made her way to the front door.

"Kiarra, where are you going?"

"Somewhere I'm wanted. To my condo."

"Come back!" He said it with more force than he intended.

Kiarra spun on her heel. "Why should I?"

"Because we're having a conversation." The truth was, he hated watching her leave each time.

"So, what?" came her flippant response.

Grinning, he walked to the door and barricaded her exit. "Simple question. Do you have conversations with people in the other condos?"

"Why? It bothers you?" She gave him a dry grin.

"You're not getting past this door. So, you might have to throw yourself out of the window after all."

She laughed, hitting her hand against the wall. Then, she strode in, and dropped her bag on the grey three-cushion sofa.

"That's the last time you'll call me intrusive, Ryder."

"OK. That's the last time you'll call me gloomy."

Kiarra kissed her teeth.

Pointing to her full lips, he shook his head. "Or kiss your teeth. I hate it."

"What? I grew up doing that. You can't expect me to just quit kissing my teeth in one day."

"Try. You'll get brownie points for effort."

She giggled. "Oh, so you listen to what I say?"

"I made pancakes, didn't I?"

"True. You followed my recipe correctly."

"You ordered me to make you pancakes. No woman has ever done that. Not even my mom."

She shrugged. "They didn't try hard enough."

"No. You're different."

"Of course, I'm different. I'm Kiarra Wright."

"This is when you also say, Ryder, you're different."

"Ah, no. But you've got a mouth."

He chuckled, dropping into his open-ended sofa. "Where's home for you?"

She went to stand by the window and stared out. He wondered why she felt the need to put some space between them?

"I'm from Detroit, Michigan."

"I've never been lucky with southern women."

Her head whirled back to him. "Have you ever dated a black woman before?"

"Are all southern women black?"

"Smarty pants, you got me there. So, you've never dated a black woman. Got it."

"That's not what I said. How's this about me? I asked the question. Tell me about your mom."

"Ah-ah! The fact you opened up today doesn't mean I've got to do the same thing."

He sat upright to face her. "What are you doing? Are you shutting down now?"

"Yes. Finding you in bed with Hailey doesn't exactly fill me with excitement and pleasant memories."

"Don't tell me you're jealous."

She averted her gaze. "If I were jealous, it would mean I was interested in you, which I'm not."

"Right. If you're not interested in me, why do you care whether, or not I eat healthy, or remain gloomy?"

"So, you think I care about you because I want to sleep with you?"

"Those are your words, not mine. I know you won't sleep with me if I were the last man on earth, right?"

"Right!"

Her rejection stirred him into action. He leaped off the sofa and took four long strides to stand beside her.

"Do you mean that?" His pulse raced.

"Of course," she said, turning up her oval face to stare at him with wistful eyes that wrenched his heart.

"Do I look like Hailey?"

"Not at all. That's why I can't shake you off."

"Don't worry I'll make it easier for you. I'll shake myself off."

By now, he stood so close, he saw her dark pupils enlarge before the pair went into hiding beneath her black lashes. Her long, straight nose begged for a kiss, and so did her cupid's bow lip.

"What's going on with you, Kiarra? For someone who isn't jealous, you've got a lot of beef with me over who I sleep with. Be honest, it bothers you."

"It doesn't!"

As she tore herself away from him, he clamped her shoulders and stirred her back.

"Want me to kiss you? Is that what this is about?"

She gasped and her eyes flipped back to his own. No matter what she said, her parted lips extended an open invitation to him. And her glistening white teeth was the icing on the cake.

Feeling a whirl of potent emotions through his spine, he inclined his head and claimed her lips with his own.

Pleasure exploded right through him.

His neighbour moaned at length, pressing her soft curves against his hard frame until he vibrated with repressed longing.

With both hands, he gathered her closer, wanting to feel every inch of her delightful stature. He teased her super-soft, moist bottom lip, nipped the corners before sliding his tongue inside to meet hers.

A hundred stars twinkled in his heart. He groaned with agonizing desire.

He felt Kiarra's hands clench his waist while she swung her tongue around the insides of his mouth.

To his fulfilment, she shuddered in his arms, an echo of the cyclone skating through his spine.

The casual warmth welling up inside him for weeks sparked into a flame, scalded his chest and powered down to his groin. He flicked his tongue around her lips, and caressed her tongue again until both of them stopped for a breather.

Before he could say anything else, Kiarra grabbed her bag and fled from his condo.

Chapter 6 – Booty Call

Kiarra

Back from the movie theater the following Saturday night, Kiarra unlocked her condo front door.

"Next time, I'm picking the movie, seriously. Your movie choice was a flop tonight," Zack Crater, her companion for the evening, concluded, his tone sardonic.

Kiarra rolled her eyes at her friend, who did not notice because he was more interested in adjusting the collar of his black leather jacket.

"Come on, Zack. Don't I get a free pass for one bad pick?" She pushed the door open and avoided his mocking grey eyes.

Zack moved past her and walked ahead, brushing one fair hand across his side-parted hay haircut.

"No, you don't." Chuckling, he added. "When I picked an awful meal for us to try in January, did you give me a free pass?"

Along the hallway, Kiarra stopped to remove her scarf and hung it on the hook. She patted down her navy, art deco evening dress. "Let's face it, I'm better at choosing our meals."

"What the freak?" Zack woofed from the living room. "Who are you?" she heard him ask.

Alarmed, Kiarra rushed forward, and ground to a halt when she got to her living room. Her heart jolted.

Dressed in a khaki long-sleeve shirt over black denim with a pair of dark loafers snuggling his feet, Ryder Blade clasped his hands over one crossed knee. Poised, he sat like a king on her sapphire blue three-cushion seater, facing the floor-to-ceiling glass windows. The curtains had been pulled apart, so dimming natural light combined with the overhead chandelier illumination to cast a halo around his faux hawk dark brown hair.

All the horny feelings from their first kiss one week ago flooded her body with rapid speed.

Ryder raised one mysterious eyebrow. "Hi Zack. I'm her loving boyfriend. I came to see my babe."

Kiarra's jaw slackened as excitement spun through her head. *Did Ryder just claim to be my boyfriend?*

"Kiarra? You've got a boyfriend?" Zack queried his tone accusatory as he turned around to face her.

"Don't listen to him," she scoffed after she found her voice. "He's Ryder Blade, my broody neighbour."

Ryder stood and paraded around her square glass coffee table. He then strode between two single scalloped velvet arm chairs as if they co-signed the lease for the condo. One look at his toned ass and legs defined in his outfit and her boobs felt heavier. Not to mention his muscles outlined in his shape-fitting top.

Her chest thundered with mixed emotions. It was amazing to find him seated in her home. But it was also a huge shock. Her palms grew sweaty, so she rubbed it over her knee-length dress shaping her hips

"Oh. When did you move in, new neighbour?" Zack quizzed, tearing his head in Ryder's direction, totally unaware of any undercurrent.

He went over to Ryder and extended his hand. That was a friendly gesture. Thankfully, Ryder accepted the handshake.

"I'm her boyfriend. If she hasn't mentioned me yet, then she's hiding something from you."

A soft punch landed in her gut. Ryder was paying her back for what she did to Hailey at his condo.

Zack retuned his gaze to Kiarra. "What's going on?"

"How did you even get my keys, Ryder?" That was the starting point. Many questions raced through her mind. "And what are you doing here?"

"That's not what you said when you kissed me a week ago at my place," Ryder mocked, casting a wink.

Zack's jaw dropped. "What the hell?" he blustered after he composed himself.

Across the room, Kiarra pierced Ryder with bold eyes. "Did I kiss you? You kissed me. That's the truth."

"It was a truly passionate kiss. My lips still burn," Ryder emphasized, chuckling in her face.

"I'm confused." Zack cleared his throat. "Are you dating your neighbour, Kiarra?"

"Of course," Ryder insisted, narrowing his eyes.

"Of course not!" she denied hotly, speaking at the same time as Ryder.

"Looks like I'm interrupting some unfinished business," Zack said after an awkward interval. "Let me know when you're done with him, Kiarra, or you can ask him to leave us alone."

"I'm done," she insisted, gritting her teeth. What did Ryder think he was doing?

Her neighbour persisted. "That's not what you say to me when you spend time at my home, every week."

"Do you spend time at his home, Kiarra?" Zack's grey eyes widened in shock. "Every week?"

"Yes, but it's not what you think. I was only help–"

"Well, I'm not ready to share you with Zack, or anyone else. That's our deal," Ryder interrupted.

Zack shook his head. "Unbelievable! Is he your neighbour, or boyfriend? Be honest with me."

"Ryder, we don't have a deal and you know it," she contradicted in a shaky voice. *Why am I caving in?*

"Then what do you call what we have? An affair between two needy hearts?" her neighbour posited. "Tell him the truth, babe."

"If this is what you want, Kiarra, say so. Ours is straightforward. If either of us fall for someone else, we speak up and move on. Is this it?"

Though Zack's words were barely above a whisper, his tone sounded pained. She did not blame him for been disappointed in her.

"I'm sorry I blind-sided you with this." Those were the only confident words that came out of her mouth.

Zack drew closer and tucked her stray curls behind her ears. Involuntarily, she tensed inside. In fact, her stomach muscles recoiled. Did her body reject, Zack's touch because of her gloomy neighbour's dirty look? *Lord! What's going on with me?*

"What are you saying, Kiarra? Is Ryder the one?"

"I already told you all you need to know," pushy Ryder replied after a lengthy pause.

"Maybe I don't know, Zack. Is that good enough?"

Zack cupped her face and kissed her lips. She did not feel an overriding urge to tease his lips, or skate tongue-to-tongue. Anyway, it was soon over.

"That's the last time you'll ever kiss, Kiarra," Ryder spoke up from behind her. "I don't share my girl."

Kiarra froze as Ryder's voice pounded behind her neck. His fragranced body heat sheltered her in a secure cape she did not want to break–ever.

"The only person who matters in this conversation is Kiarra. Don't break her heart, Ryder. Don't emotionally abuse her, or make her feel less than beautiful. She's my girl. If things don't work out between you two, I'll replace you without a second thought. Do you get me?" Zack met Ryder's gaze.

"You won't get a second chance," Ryder spoke across her shoulder, but he did not touch her.

From her head to her toes, she shuddered inwardly.

Zack shrugged. "Time will tell. Kiarra, take care of yourself. I'll see myself out."

The spell around her shattered at Zack's final remark. She then hurried after him.

"Thank you for your understanding, Zack. When I figure out what's going on with me, I'll let you know, I promise."

Her friend nodded. "It's complicated, I see that."

"Yes, it is," she confessed. "Speak soon."

"Bye, Kiarra."

"Goodbye, Zack."

After she locked the door, Kiarra marched to the living room. She found Ryder staring out of her glass window, a mirror image of her posture a week ago in his condo.

"What are you doing here, Ryder Blade? Whatever you think is going on between us is over! How did I go from being rejected by you to being your *babe*, hmm?"

With his hands thrust into his denim pockets, he kept his back to her.

"I came to see you."

"You moved into *Cable Point Condos* three months ago, why now? Why tonight?"

"You fled after I kissed you. That told me a lot."

"Oh! But that's not what you told, Zack." The mere mention that his lips caressed hers still tickled her.

"We'll come back to Zack. After I kissed you–" his eyes steadied on hers as if he wanted her to make a second request to have his virile lips turn her emotions upside down, again.

"–I waited for a whole week to see you. When you didn't use your key to let yourself inside my condo, I showered, got ready and showed up at the monthly house barbecue party. But you weren't there."

She shrugged. "So, what? I've got a life."

"That's not what you told me when I first moved in. You said everyone attended the monthly parties for a reason–to catch up and to be there for each other. Why did you skip the party today?"

"As you clearly saw, I was out on a date with Zack."

Ryder curved his lithe body with his arms folded across the expanse of his chest. His bulky arms fought against his T-shirt sleeves as if the muscles would rip through the seams with brute force.

Aroused, she brushed her eyes over his thighs and legs highlighted from every angle in his denim pants. His top and jeans stretched tight around his sinewy physique leaving little to her imagination.

"No one at the party knew where you were. You gave me an impression you all knew everything about each other. Found out that wasn't true."

"Guess I wasn't in the mood to answer awkward questions since I wasn't sure you'd show up there."

Standing with Ryder Blade inside her condo was surreal. She was still in a bit of shock.

"Awkward questions about me?" He waggled one brow. She pinned her lips together to avoid grinning.

"Yes." She broke her gaze from his own and crossed the hardwood floor toward her open plan kitchen.

"Were you worried they'll figure out you've got a thing for me?" He did not move from where he stood.

Ryder was baiting her, but she would not bite.

"Did you have fun at the barbecue party?"

"No. You weren't there, so it was not the same."

His tone had a rough edge, he almost sounded like he missed her. But she found that hard to believe.

"I'm not the life of the party, Ryder."

"Everyone missed you. They think I'm the reason you didn't show up. Is it true?"

To avoid replying, she reached for the kettle. From her side, Ryder's hand pressed on hers.

Gasping, she dragged in a long breath.

"Take your hands off. I want to make coffee."

"Not until you tell me why you're running away from me. You kissed me back with enough passion to light up this entire country. That kind of passion doesn't fade away in one week for no reason."

Her pulse jumped all over the place and her heart thudded. "You've not given me one reason to stay."

"Don't run away from me, from us." He stroked the back of her hand.

"There's no *us*. I can't do this with you, Ryder." She wanted to dry out the slushy feeling inside her belly.

"Why not?"

He stood so close she felt his breath on her forehead. Even his sexy cologne accessed her pores.

"Because you'll break my heart. You've got nothing to give me, or Hailey, or any other woman in your closed life. Your heart is empty. Your mood swings drive me insane. I don't want to die before my time."

His hand stiffened on top of hers for a moment, before he relaxed and caressed the back of her hand with the pad of his fingers again.

Coals burned up her arms. Heat scalded her cleavage and left her nipples raw with need. Night after night, she had longed for his touch and his bad boy kisses. Yet, standing close to him now, she trembled.

"Kiarra Wright, you keep it real like no other woman I've ever met. You're right. My heart was empty. Not anymore. I met you and with every visit you made to my condo you filled my heart with hope, with new possibilities, laughter, and many other strange but great emotions."

Her pulse ticked loud and fast. Was she dreaming? Her heart beat very strong and out of her chest. She darted her tongue over her lip with nervous pleasure.

Frankly, she had not expected him to open up to her, or to be vulnerable. Slowly, she lifted her head, so she could stare into his eyes.

Eyes never lied. His hazel pair opened up to hers for the first time. He did not try to cover up his feelings, or hide behind harsh, dismissive words.

"Let's start over, Kiarra. Please. I'll treat you right, Miss Wright. I'll learn how."

Tremors crashed inside her stomach. And, a soft giggle staggered out of her lips. Ryder had finally succumbed to his feelings.

Feelings she did not know he concealed from her.

The wall she had put up around her heart after their first kiss a week ago toppled over before her eyes.

"Dating you is a big risk, Ryder Blade. I'll be putting my heart on the line for a man who's proven to me he's incapable of giving me anything back."

He squeezed her hand gently. "I'm sorry, I made you feel that way. I wasn't looking for any of this and I didn't think for a moment I'd fall for a woman from Detroit. When I'm with you, I feel like I'm back home, the time I'd some great memories."

The words from his mouth soothed away her angst.

"When you kissed me, I knew the truth I'd been fighting for a while."

"And you knew I'd found out you were into me. That scared you." He interpreted her pause correctly.

"A lot. I was mortified."

"So mortified, you were willing to give up having fun with your friends tonight at the barbecue party."

"Yeah. I didn't want anyone to tease me about you. When I kissed you back, I gave up everything I'd been hiding from you. I was embarrassed."

"It's nothing to be ashamed of because it took that kiss for me to admit I was falling for you. I thought I'd get over the way I felt in one day. But in the last seven days, all I've wanted was to see you, to talk to you, to kiss you some more. Once wasn't enough."

He lifted his other hand to her face, scooped her neck and dunked his head.

"Give me the chance to earn the right to ask you, personal questions. Be my babe."

All shades of sweetness filled her body.

Meanwhile, he perched his tongue at the corner of her lips, making her wait for the tongue locking. There was nothing she could say, or do. Her heart juggled inside her chest. She wanted this, but he could hurt her with a single remark, or his famed frosty attitude.

While she delayed her response, Ryder cupped his mouth over hers in a potent, passionate plea.

Blissful shocks vibrated across her boobs and entire body. She curled her fingers around his forearms and pressed closer to him. He freed her hand and pulled her closer until she stretched flat against his granite frame. Current whirred between their tongues and lips. Gross heat charged between their skins. In that moment, something wild and wonderful happened. She no longer remembered why she was hesitant.

When Ryder paused their kiss, his fingers still cuddled her face. Their heads touched. Her heartbeat raced on. She grasped his arms with her hands, holding on, so she remained steady on jittery legs.

"What do you really want from me, Ryder Blade?"

"Give me a chance to show you, I'm serious. It's the least you owe me for the many months you crept into my condo with keys I didn't give to you."

Laughter built up in her gut and rolled out.

"Let me think about it," she told him afterward.

Her answer was an easy one, but she had to act like she needed time to ponder to maintain her dignity.

"For the sake of transparency and full disclosure, I want to say I didn't have sex with, Hailey the day you barged into my bedroom."

She arched her neck. "What was she doing in her underwear and with her legs twined around yours?"

"When I called her, that was my intention–to have casual sex. That's the truth. But when she arrived, all I talked about was you."

He caressed her cheek with the side of his thumb. It felt right. It felt delightful.

"And she simply listened?"

It was hard for her trust what he said because she had seen the scene herself. In fact, she was sure the room smelled of sex that morning.

"Yeah, she did. I didn't sleep with her. I'm being honest." He pulled out his cell phone from his denim pocket. "Take. Call her. Ask her whatever you want."

"Why would I do that? She was your booty call before that day anyway. I'm not going to speak with a woman who's had sex with you on many occasions."

"True. But that was before I met you. It was how I coped. It was how I escaped getting involved in something deep and meaningful."

"Why would she listen to you talk about me?" Hailey must be a saint. She would have knocked off his teeth instead of listening to him chat on.

"It was the first time she'd heard me carry on about another woman. I guess she was intrigued."

"And she wasn't offended?"

"Not in the least. We've not got an emotional bond. What about, Zack?" He did not stop petting her cheek.

She averted her gaze.

Ryder turned her chin with his fingers so she could not hide. "Is he someone I should worry about?"

"Mm-hmm."

His lips thinned and, the Adam apple at his neck throbbed. It was a sign he was pissed. Too bad.

"What do you have going on with Zack?"

She shrugged. "We're friends with benefits."

Now his eyes darkened. "For how long?"

"Over two years. And Hailey? How long has she been on your booty call list?"

"Three years. Why do I need to worry about, Zack?"

"I've got a soft spot for him. He's nice, caring, dependable. Kind of like a cozy blanket."

Frankly, she loved this aspect of their budding affair. Being open and honest was all she ever asked from any man she dated.

"Maybe tone down his perfect attributes. Don't need to know. The guy's in love with you. Did you know that?"

"He's not!" she denied. Zack was not in love with her. Their relationship was not an emotional one in that sense. They were good friends who seldom hit the sack. When they did, it was to scratch their itch.

"Great. I'm relieved you didn't figure that out. Like I told Zack, I'm not willing to share you with him. Break it off with Mr. Nice. His time in your life is over, Kiarra. Mine is just starting and, I don't see an end."

Wow! Her stomach walls coiled with delicious sparks. She angled her head and blinked. *Excuse me?*

"Where's this ferocious personality coming from, Ryder Blade? I didn't think you had it in you."

"Well, you thought wrong. You've awakened something hot, powerful and territorial inside me. I'm not letting you go. Get me?"

Moaning softly against his bearded jawline, she twisted her mouth, so her eyes hovered around his attractive lips. Nothing he said changed the fact she wanted another kiss from him. His lips were a weapon designed to unleash mass pleasure on her whole body. And she was now an addict.

Inhaling sharply, she sneaked her hands up to his neck, slipped them through his silky hair and massaged his scalp. He bowed his head and pushed nearer to her face. With her lips upturned, she hoped he knew what she wanted without her saying nothing.

Ryder Blade plugged her mouth with his own just the way she needed it. When his tongue tickled hers, it was as if he added coals to burning coals, and wood to fire for as long as the intense kiss lasted.

He eased his mouth off hers and trailed down to her chin muttering, "I want to take you out next weekend. Plan to be out with me for a couple of hours. My treat. I intend to make up for my bad ways."

Arching her neck, she grinned. "Time?"

"Five."

"What do I wear? Formal? Casual? Sporty? Where are we going?"

A sexy grin marked his already striking features. "Wear what makes you happy. Blow my mind."

Electric heat coursed through her cleavage. She leaned inward, curved her neck and caught his lips with hers.

"Gloomy but brazenly sexy and handsome, Ryder Blade now intends to date me?"

Standing with his iron hands wrapped around her and his mouth showing her a passionate new world, this was more than she ever fantasized. A man built like a sex hero with a sharp six-pack that Nick Bateman would envy had never even looked her way, much more asked her out to have drinks.

"I'm not gloomy anymore. We agreed. The answer to that is a big, yeah!"

Just to be sure she was not in an imaginary land she drifted her fingers along his neck and massaged his macho chest with her palms. Casually. His chest pounded. Rigid muscles, warm to her touch, flexed.

Parting her lips, she tilted her head.

Warmth altered his eyes from the usual melancholic hazel to a merry green shade.

"I love your eyes, boyfriend. They tell me your mood. They're brilliant and intense right now."

He nipped her bottom lip. "And that means what?"

"You enjoy kissing me and you long for me."

Chuckling, he caught her top lip between his teeth. "Didn't I say that from the moment I walked in?"

Breathing in his fragrance, she snatched his lips with her mouth and ended his teasing torture.

After that, she caught sight of several paper bags lying behind her sofa. How did she miss the whole lot?

"Did you bring me those paper bags?"

He smooched her lips with his own. "Check them after I'm gone."

"Aw...thank you."

"Don't thank me. It's nothing much."

"Whatever you've got in those bags, I appreciate them, Ryder."

"You deserve a lot more, Kiarra Wright. Did I tell you how beautiful you look tonight? My chest was pounding when I saw you."

Giggling, she fluttered her lashes. "Not yet."

"I'll show you."

Nothing felt more amazing than to have the man she wanted most in the world whisper sweet words in her ear on a Saturday night in the middle of June.

Chapter 7 – Say More

Ryder

Ryder regarded his outfit with a keen eye through the full-length mirror in his bedroom.

His heart thundered against his chest for a bit.

Straightening the collar of his starched white dress shirt, he angled his head. With quick strokes, he patted the sides of his faux hawk hairstyle. Then he gave a nervous laugh to his mirror image.

"It's our first date," he mumbled. "Calm down."

Ryder licked his lips dry and then coughed out air from his mouth. He then tossed one mint candy inside his mouth. Nothing must go wrong tonight.

"Why am I so fucking nervous?" Ryder asked his reflection. "Because I don't want to blow it with Kiarra!" he answered himself.

You won't, his inner self spoke up.

Assured at last, he sprayed another layer of perfume at his pulse points and clipped on his gold wristwatch. He stared at his crease-free tailored dark pants and polished black shoes. Intending not to keep his date waiting, he grabbed her gift and made his way out of his condo. If only his heart would stop singing out loud. He hoped today's date went as he planned–hitch-free from start to end.

At the front of Kiarra's door, he paused. Shaky a little, he bent his neck back and stared at the ceiling.

"I can do this," he murmured.

Taking a deep breath, he rapped on Kiarra's door. Before he could take in another long breath, the door opened more than a fraction.

And his jaw pulled wide apart, he had to pick it up from the floor.

"Damn hot, babe!"

A red tulle gown crafted Kiarra's curves in a way that made his groin ache. The sweeping dress with a plunging neckline accentuated her sleekly-full boobs. His eyes stationed at the spot between her cleavage for seconds before dipping to her not-so-slim waist held tight by a gold belt. The soft fabric flowed over her belly, broad hips and legs, settling around her feet in a splendid red pool. Her hair, now untwisted had exploded into a bouncy, dark golly of curls.

"Please tell me you're blown away?" she asked in an unsteady sweet voice.

Grinning, he took a few steps forward, caught her waist with one hand and hugged her tight.

"Of course, I'm blown away! I'm speechless."

As his fingers crawled around her back, he found out her gown was completely backless except for two strings crossing at the centre of her back.

"Are you kidding? My elegant Kiarra, you look so incredible I feel like I don't deserve you as my date."

She sighed. "Really? I'm glad you're impressed."

Kiarra Wright was gorgeous, period. This woman was a far cry in appearance from the one who often wore oversized t-shirts and jeans to his condo.

With his pulse still leaping, he leaned his jaw on her neck and breathed in her unbelievable scent.

"You smell so good, Kiarra. I'm totally blown away."

She giggled softly.

"Thank you. Careful. I don't want to stain your white shirt. Ryder Blade, you clean up good. My heart is pumping really fast."

He chuckled in her ear. "I strived to impress you."

A broad smile formed across his face. It felt great to hear her say she noticed he made an effort. Because he did. It took him longer than necessary to put his outfit together—for her.

"You sure did. You look like a delicious candy."

Wild laughter rocked his chest. "This is for you." He handed over the bouquet of fresh flowers after that.

"It smells so lovely, Ryder. Thank you."

She blinked a few times. It was then he noted her lovely deep-brown eyes, lined with black ink and her beautifully made-up face. Cheeks more defined with pink blusher and her full-bodied lips coloured a dark red aroused his senses. Her straight, dark eyebrows arched toward the end combined to enhance the beauty of her oval face.

Lifting her head from inhaling the bouquet scent, Kiarra giggled. "Scented red roses. How did you know I love these?"

He shrugged. "Took a wild guess."

In more ways than one, Kiarra reminded him of the actress, Simone Missick, but his babe was even more stunning.

"Come inside," she said going ahead. "Let me put these babies in water. I'm so happy right now."

Following her inside, he stood in the centre of her living room, watching her glide toward the kitchen.

"Your condo is a lovely warm space. Is blue your best colour?" It was interesting how her condo was mainly a white and blue themed décor.

"Actually yes. I love blue, every shade of it. What about you? What's your number one colour?"

"Grey any day."

"Ah. You sure do. I'm going to need a huge vase." She raided the storage cupboards. "How many roses did you get for me, Ryder?"

"Fifty. Too many?" He was not sure if he had overdone it. *Better more than less*, he reckoned.

She flashed him a stunning smile. "Never too many. I love every single one of these red roses. Beautiful, and they smell like bliss. Thank you very much."

Great start. Nodding, he mentally patted his back.

Ten minutes later, he held the Bentley car door open for her outside their condo building.

Before Kiarra entered the car, she stared up at him and gave him a hot grin. "I feel like a princess."

"More than that, you're my queen, Kiarra."

His heart picked up pace, jumped and skidded. Inside the car, at the backseat moments later, she reached for his hand. Thrilled, he threaded his fingers with hers as they locked gazes.

"Where are we going?" Her question came after a long, awareness powered pause.

"We're going on a ride."

"A ride? This is a luxury car ride already."

Chuckling, he shook his head. "That's all you need to know until we get there."

Raising one eyebrow, she smiled. "Get where?"

"Let's talk about something else. Have you ever been married before?"

Kiarra shut her eyes before bursting into a really cute laugh.

"What?" he queried, grinning himself.

"No. I've not been lucky enough for a guy I love to go down on one knee. What about you? Any wife I need to know about?"

"None. I'm not the marrying type."

She jerked her head back, her fingers trapped in his own stiffened.

"Excuse me?" Her eyes snagged his own.

"Wrong answer." With a fix in mind, he raised one hand. "Let me rephrase that. I've not found the one."

"Makes more sense." His girlfriend nodded in approval, accepting his second answer.

Be careful, his inner voice warned. He almost punched his mouth for speaking out of turn.

"Something you said still bothers me, Ryder."

"What is it? Ask away."

"Why did you need a booty call to escape? What do you need to escape from?"

"Let it go, Kiarra. I don't want to rehash the past."

Shaking her head, she honed her gaze on him.

"I can't, Ryder." She spoke softly. "If I want to get to know you, that's where I want to start."

"Please, Kiarra. This date is special because you're with me and it's our first. Can we enjoy it, for us?"

"OK. You owe me an explanation."

Chuckling, he placed his arm across his chest.

"That I do. I know I will, in time. Not now."

"Fine. Where are you from, Ryder?"

Relieved to move on to easy questions, he relaxed against the leather interior seat. "Denver, Colorado."

"Hmm. You've got the Rocky Mountains nearby."

"Yeah. Denver is the famous jumping-off point for the ski resorts in the Rocky Mountains."

"Do you ski?"

"A lot when I was growing up. I've not done any skiing in years. Do you ski?"

"Not really. But if you count watching others ski on TV from my couch, I've got a lot of experience."

Tickled red by her response, he exploded with laughter. For several minutes, he shook beside his date and knocked his elbow against the door handle. While he laughed, Kiarra watched him, smiling and snapping a few shots of him with her cell phone.

"Let's take a selfie," she requested when he gave her cell phone a pointed look.

"I dislike taking pictures," he protested. His photos must not make it to social media.

But Kiarra shifted, so her head rested on his chest as she lifted the camera in her hand at an angle.

"Smile," she told him, giggling.

He gave his best brooding gaze instead of a sharp smile. Not bothered by his menacing stare, Kiarra clicked the side button of her cell phone. Of course, her smile was red-carpet worthy. She took three shots, altering her pose with each one.

When she sat upright again, he wished she had not. Her body had steamed his briefly. It felt great. The flimsy strands of her gown revealed the smooth goodness of her deep brown skin. Natural light burrowing past the window sheets warmed her arms and shoulders to an umber tint that reminded him of the delicious golden-brown pancakes she made for him weeks ago.

"What else is Denver known for, Ryder?"

"Actually, my parents' home is close to Molly Brown's mansion. And, I'm not name dropping."

Fine lines creased her otherwise smooth brow. "Molly Brown?"

"Yeah. The same one."

"The titanic survivor, Molly Brown?" Her mouth cupped into an attractive O as she gulped in air.

"Yeah. Our houses are like two miles apart."

"That's awesome! Then, how did you end up here in San Diego?"

"First, school. Then I stayed for work."

Her eyes glowed as she asked her next question. "What school?"

"University of San Diego for my graduate degree. I started out reading Finance. But I quickly switched to Business Administration. Did you get your degree in Detroit?"

"Yeah. Studied sociology in Oakland University, Michigan."

"Impressive. What then drew you from Detroit to the Grape State?"

"Adventure I guess."

"What kind of adventure?"

She hesitated. The pause was long enough to bring them to Montgomery Drive, the location of *Corporate Helicopters* building in central San Diego.

Gasping, Kiarra squeaked. "A helicopter ride?"

"Please don't say you're acrophobic. I should've asked you first. I just assumed–"

Covering her mouth with both hands, she shook her head, cutting off his words. "Don't worry. I'm not afraid of heights in the least. But I'm in shock." She started to giggle, making wonderful sound in his ear.

Cuddling her hands, he uncovered her face.

"Good shock, I hope."

"Of course. I've never been in one." Her eyes bulged with excitement.

"Phew! That's amazing news, yeah. We're going on a helicopter tour of San Diego. Should we get down?"

"Yes please."

For the next forty minutes, or more they flew around the bustling city. Coloured city lights waved at them from below. Beside him, Kiarra clung to his upper arm with one hand while she peered out of the window. As they flew past *Belmont Park*, the historic amusement park, *Presidio Park* at Ocean Front and *Point Loma*, a rugged peninsula famous for Cabrillo National Monument with tide pools and trails, he pointed out each landmark to his girlfriend.

Laughing, she chatted and asked many questions.

He flagged one more of the city's landmarks. "That's *Solana Beach* right there. Ever been there?"

"Oh yeah. It's very nice. Have you been there?"

"A few times."

"This is so incredible, Ryder! I love the aerial view of a city I've lived in for a while."

"I'm glad. How long have you been in San Diego?"

Of course, they had to raise their voices above the whirring rotors to hear each other.

"A little over two years now," she told him.

"Oh, so you're still pretty new to the city."

"You could say that."

It felt surreal to have her cling to him in the confined space. Every now and then, his eyes flashed to her thigh peeking out from the slit on her gorgeous gown. Super-tanned skin with traces of cellulite flirted with him. Normally, he would have been turned off at the first sight of a cellulite thighs. On Kiarra however, it looked appealing. He did not care at all.

"One question is pending. What adventure drew you to the Land of Milk and Honey, Kiarra?"

"Zack told me about a job opportunity here, so I applied and I was offered the job. It's a trendier city than Detroit of course."

"Ah, so we both left our home cities for job opportunities here. Would you call that fate?" It irked him, her move to the city was Zack's idea. On the other hand, he was grateful for the chance to date her.

"More like God's plan. Maybe. We'll see."

Somehow, he did not believe she was being totally open about why she moved to San Diego. Moments before they arrived at the helipad, she had said adventure brought her to the city.

"Was it an adventure, or work that got you here?"

"Both. I'd a nasty break up six months prior, so the timing to change cities was perfect for me."

Now he felt like a jerk for pushing for an answer. "Glad you're here," he told her clasping her hand. "That's the coastline between Oceanside and Del Mar." He motioned to the view in sight.

"Stunning view from up here, honestly."

"Want to head to Los Angeles?"

Juddering beside him, Kiarra drew in a long breath and tightened her fingers around his arm.

"What? We're flying to LA now?"

He laughed at the glee on her beautiful face.

"Yeah. We're heading there right now."

No amount of money would be too much to spend to see her look so happy. This was the most romantic experience he had set up in a long time and he was pleased she loved the experience.

"Wow!" She peered up at him. "Thank you for this. Nothing else matters. I love this, Ryder."

He caressed her right thigh, not the one with the slit. Though he wished he was seated on her left side.

"Tell me, did you always want to be a sales guy?" she queried, redirecting her gaze out of the window.

There was something he needed to tell her about his job, but now was not the time.

"You could say that. I've always had an interest in sales. Although I started out in operations, then corporate social responsibility before I ended in sales. Selling is everything. If you don't sell, you don't make money. Simple."

"I get that. So, how do you convince customers to buy, *Rich Earth Coffee*?"

"By trying to understand customer needs. The only way to do that is to be out in the field, where the customers make buying decisions."

She nodded. "Makes perfect sense. So how do you influence customers to choose your product?"

He chuckled. "Want me to give up my secret?"

"Mm-hmm. Maybe. In a way, we all buy and sell. I'd like to know how to sell more."

"What do you do? It's strange I've never asked."

Grinning, she gestured at the natural vegetation zones in the distance. "That's *Balboa Park*. The Zoo."

"Yeah."

"I thought so. What a pretty view from here," she gushed, leaning toward the window.

As a result, she inadvertently dragged him with her. He ducked his head to stare at the view himself. Shaking her head afterward, she sighed.

"I don't want this to end, Ryder."

His heart jerked hard in his chest. Feeling quite emotional, he cupped her face with his fingers.

Kiarra gasped gently.

In that moment, he knew she was beautiful inside and out. Her lips split apart and she dipped her eyelashes. Heat seared his chest and rushed upward to his mouth.

Grunting from the aching need trapped in his groin, he crushed her mouth with his own. She curled her hands around his neck and savoured his lips with her tongue. Blood rang in his ears. He was sure she could hear the sound as his body quivered with need.

"Kiarra Wright, you've swept me off my feet," he whispered against her mouth minutes later. He felt his neck and face flush with heat.

Pretty lines framed her eyes as she giggled.

"Never have I heard that line before. You've blown me off my feet too, Ryder Blade. You really have and I'm more than impressed."

"Good to know we feel the same way about each other. Something just occurred to me."

She pulled back and smiled. "What is it?"

"Let's play the game, Never Have I."

Kiarra crinkled her eyes and nose as she stared at him. "I'll go first. Never have I lied to you."

"Good. Never have I kissed anyone half my age."

Kiarra dissolved in giggles. "Never Have I dated anyone twice my age."

He grinned, completely in awe of his date. "Never Have I stolen anything.

"OK. Never Have I proposed to anyone before you."

He winked. "Never Have I peed in the pool."

Laughing, she shook her head. "Okay, we're done."

"To be continued," he agreed, laughing with her.

She squeezed his hand. "Have you got family in San Diego?"

Current burned his skin and he slowly turned red. Kiarra made him feel amazing things. Every touch, every look deepened their connection.

"None."

"Have you got brothers, sisters?"

"One sister, Alana. She's older. Alana's in next door state, in Nevada. She lives in Las Vegas, works as an interior design consultant and a brand ambassador. She's almost married."

"*Almost married*? Was she engaged?"

"He cancelled on the wedding day. Just kidding."

"You got me there. I was going to say that's awful."

He shrugged. "Wanted to throw that in."

"That's a crazy joke. Do you see, Alana often?"

"Not as much as I would like, but Alana's a big girl. And you? Any brothers I should be worried about?"

"Yeah. I've got an older sister too, Jalicia who's a science teacher, lives in New Jersey. She's three years older than Deiondre, my brother. He's two years older than me and he's a bank manager in Atlanta, Georgia."

"Looks like you all decided to spread your wings across the country. How often do you get to see your siblings?"

"We talk over video call when we're free. I speak with, Deiondre more when he's not caught up in the craziness of the financial world. Jalicia's students are her first priority and I've got a life I like here. But we're all really close. My family's everything to me."

"Put a figure to the ages. How old are you?"

"Like I told you before, thirty-one in early August."

"Okay. That makes, Jalicia thirty-six and Deiondre's thirty-three."

"You've got it figured out. We usually meet for Thanksgiving every year. Is my sister older than you?"

"By a year. I'll be thirty-five next month. On the twentieth. I've not had a sit-down Thanksgiving dinner in however long. I can't even remember."

"Seriously? You're a July baby? And you don't do Thanksgiving dinner? I should invite you to mine. It's when we catch up on each other's lives. Always fun."

He laughed. "Is that what I'm called?"

"Mm-hmm. July baby. Independence Day, duh!"

No one, in fact no woman had called him *baby* as long as he could remember. Tingling heat lined his spine. Kiarra did not even call him *baby*. She had said *you're a July baby*, yet it made him feel so good.

"Meeting family is a big deal, Kiarra. Are you sure that's a good idea? Thanksgiving dinner is huge."

Studying him with a direct gaze, she nodded.

"It's the perfect opportunity if we're still dating."

Pausing for a while to visualize the months ahead without, Kiarra made his stomach crash with terror.

"I've not got plans to break up with you. Do you?"

Beaming, she kissed his lips, cutting off the tempting caress after only a brief moment.

"Not in the immediate future, Ryder."

He narrowed his gaze and stamped his lips on her neck. "Not in the forever future, Kia. I'm not going anywhere." Then he shut her up with a kiss.

Giggling, she pecked his bicep afterward. "Good to know you're emotionally available long term. Tell me, what have you got planned for your birthday?"

"Not sure." He kissed her chin before falling back on his butt. "There's nothing to celebrate, trust me."

She twisted and faced the window.

"Everyone's got a reason to celebrate, Ryder. You're alive. That's one good reason. God loves you."

"Are you mad at me? You think I'm ungrateful?"

"I'm not mad." His girlfriend swung her head back to face him and grinned. "Just an optimist who sees many reasons why we should be happy and thankful."

"Well, I'm a pragmatist," he countered. "If I've got no reason to be happy, I'm not. But right now, I've got a million reasons why I'm excited."

Her grin spread to her entire face. "Really? Does that have anything to do with your date, huh?"

Winking, he gave a casual shrug. "Not so sure."

Kiarra grabbed his shirt with both hands and pulled him forward. Of course, he went along willingly.

"Since you're not sure, I need to convince you–"

Her moving scarlet lips lured him. Caught in the circle of her allure, he leaned forward and brushed his nose past hers while he breathed on her face as he steamed her mouth with his own.

"Your lips taste like delicious nectarine, ripe and full of goodness," he whispered against her cheek.

Moaning, Kiarra parted her lips. Her fingers scratched his neck and her teeth grazed along his jaw.

Quick storm plundered his gut.

"Say more," she breathed against his neck.

"Your boobs are like two gorgeous gems. I want to wrap my mouth around your nipples to taste what I imagine is your sweet flesh."

Her fingers around his neck dropped to his chest as her breathing quickened.

The glowing sights beyond the windows were soon forgotten as he moved his lips along her shoulders.

Her skin smelled like expensive summer flowers. On his tongue, she tasted like warm honey and milk. He skimmed his lips along her collar bone. Moaning roughly, Kiarra cropped his head with both hands.

"Should I stop?" Even though he asked, he did not stop. If she wanted him to, she would have to beg.

"Mm..." Soft cries rolled out of her mouth.

As he lowered his lips to her cleavage, he crooned. "Is that a stop, or go on?" He cuddled her hips and pulled her a lot closer and she warmed him up.

"S-stop," she stuttered still whimpering.

Since he was not sure what her moaning signified, he tasted the soft swell of her breast with his tongue before bathing her breast with tender kisses.

Kiarra jolted.

Her blissful boobs bounced in his face. The ache in his groin worsened, so that he shuddered in his seat. When he exhaled, a ragged sound filled the cabin.

"Did I go too far, Kiarra?"

He needed to know he had not blown the date because he could not control his longing for her.

"No. It was perfect."

Puffing out air from his mouth, he opened his eyes.

Kiarra smiled at him, not just with her mouth. Her eyes glimmered with passion and something else.

"What is it, babe?"

"I've got butterflies. You make me feel so weird. Like, I didn't think I was going to feel this way."

He grinned, extra excited she fancied him.

"Right now, I can't explain how I feel, or what's going on here." He pointed to his abs. "My stomach keeps twitching with vibes of pleasure, I don't know."

Flipping her lashes, she shifted closer.

With the need to feel her warmth some more, he pulled her to his side with one arm across her shoulders. His girlfriend leaned her head on his chest.

And together, they watched the sun dip along Los Angeles skyline.

Chapter 8 – I Was Wet

Kiarra

"*There* are children who desperately need to feel safe and loved out there. These regular kids are easy targets for grooming and crime," Kiarra stated toward the end of her presentation to potential foster parents. "But if you open your homes to these boys and girls from different backgrounds, you can provide a safe and loving home where they feel connected till, they can go on to put down roots."

The office-based event was one of many scheduled Q & A sessions for potential foster parents.

One black woman with Bantu knots hairdo raised her hand.

Kiarra nodded. "Yes, ma'am."

"Thank you, Kiarra. If we agree to sign up as foster parents, we're a black family and we prefer to foster only black kids. It's easier to blend them in to our family. Will that be a problem?"

Stretching her neck, Kiarra quickly spied the woman's name from the name tab on the table.

"Not at all, Mrs. Baker. Do you have any other concerns?"

"None."

A dark-haired Hispanic woman raised her hand immediately after, her eyes crinkled.

"Yes, ma'am. What's your question?"

"Mine is a little different. If I were to sign up, I'd like to mix things up. Say one Hispanic, one white and one black kid. Would that be possible? Because I want the children to learn to appreciate diverse cultures."

"The children available at any given time will be discussed with the foster families on our register. Yes, you can choose children from different backgrounds as long as your home meets certain criteria."

"I have everything three kids would need. When can I sign up?"

Excitement rushed through Kiarra's spine. Recruiting foster parents through advertising, interviewing applicants, processing their applications and meeting with potential parents and families was what she loved doing. Even though it was her everyday life, she always celebrated every new family that signed up. Because it meant one deprived kid got a foster home.

"Once the event ends in twenty minutes, I'll make the application forms available. Thank you, Mrs. Rodríguez. Any more questions?"

In advertising to find foster parents and homes, Kiarra had realized that using people's names created emotional connections that built trust. She had also found it helped potential foster parents make up their minds to sign up a lot faster.

The middle-aged woman shook her head.

"Does anyone else have any more questions?"

A pale woman with chestnut hair sleeked into a tidy ponytail made eye contact before lifting her hand.

"Yes, Mrs. Bush?" Kiarra signalled to the woman.

The older woman cleared her throat and then, swallowed before speaking.

"What kind of support system do you provide for foster families who get kids who are badly behaved? Can we discipline them, or do you intervene?"

"Once your application is approved, Mrs. Bush, I'm presuming you intend to apply?" Kiarra paused to get some sort of commitment from the older woman.

"I'm considering it at the moment. I just need to know some specific things to do in case it happens."

"That's fine. You'll attend foster care training that's aimed to equip you with skills to deal with children who display a range of bad behaviour."

Mrs. Bush nodded, listening with rapt attention.

"For mild disobedience for example, you can simply ignore it," Kiarra carried on. "We however encourage foster parents to praise and offer rewards for good behaviour. Depending on their ages, children can be placed on time-out, you can remove privileges and redirect the children's attention."

"What if they throw, or break my treasured pieces, or physically abuse me? As much as I'd love to provide a safe and loving home, that kind of behaviour would break my heart. How do I know I won't be knocked back and passed from one agency to another?"

"There's a safety plan in place for such cases, Mrs. Bush. It states appropriate steps to take in–"

Kiarra's words trailed off the second she spotted a six-foot-three well-rounded look of sexiness standing by the door of the conference room. *Ryder!*

He threw her a small wave and a to-die-for grin.

Inside her chest, her heart did a disco dance and her lips went parched. She swallowed.

"Kiarra, you were saying?" Mrs. Bush intervened.

Falling back on the discussion wagon in a rush, Kiarra blinked and smiled, trying to stitch her thoughts together. It had been two weeks since her helicopter ride with Ryder and their dinner date in an upscale restaurant in Los Angeles. Though she had seen, Ryder twice in the last week, it felt incredible to get a surprise visit from him in the middle of the day.

"Kiarra?"

She heard the older woman's intrusive call.

"Yes. Pardon me, Mrs. B-bush," she stuttered. "I was saying that the safety plan leaves foster families in no doubt about what to do if they encounter a child with violent behaviour. Does that answer your question, ma'am?"

"Yes." Mrs. Bush turned her head to the back of the room. When her head returned in Kiarra's direction, the older woman grinned.

"Is the gentleman at the door hoping to foster a child as well?" Mrs. Bush asked with a knowing glint in her blue eyes.

Everyone in the room, thirty-five in total swung their heads toward the door.

Thankfully, Ryder ducked out of sight.

Relieved, Kiarra ended the session shortly after that. She stayed to chat with participants over coffee and munchies. Once the last potential applicant made her way out of the room, she packed up her folder.

But butterflies roamed around in her stomach.

"Are you always so fascinating when speaking in front of a crowd?"

A sharp gasp leaped out of her lips at the refreshing sound of his voice.

"Ryder! You almost disrupted my session. How long have you been watching?"

Leaning against the door, he crossed his legs at the ankle and his arms across his chest. His fitted tailored light-blue two-piece suit worn over a white shirt, unbuttoned three steps down, shot up his already high sexual appeal. No tie. No belt. Navy shoes completed his magnificent day look. His faux hawk hair was spikier at the top as if it had been brushed by the Friday afternoon wind.

"From the start."

Her chest exploded with joy. "What? I'd no clue."

Pushing away from the door jamb, he spread out his arms. "Do I get an exclusive warm hug for my impulsive attendance?"

"Of course!"

Discarding her folder, she lengthened her strides toward him. Her pulse doubled its pace with every step she took. Before she reached his side, Ryder rushed ahead, gathered her with his rock-hard arms and pressed her flushed against his awesome body.

Oh gosh! It felt incredible to have him show up out of the blue. And his arms around her stirred feelings similar to free falling from the top of a mountain.

"Happy to see me in the middle of your day?" he chirped in her ear.

"A million yesses! What a wonderful surprise! Always smelling so good."

From his open neck shirt, she saw his gold chain coiled around a spray of dark brown hair, coating his tattooed chest.

"I must confess something," she told him, giggling.

"What?"

"My ultimate guilty pleasure is to flick my fingers across the sprinkling of hair on your chest."

A hairy-chested man was her top pick any day over a hairless chest.

He ground his teeth together. "I'm hard now, babe."

Wow! Before she could think of a reply, he dropped his head and lapped up her lips with his mouth. He kissed her so hard she did not even remember what they were talking about.

"Touch my chest," he invited, crooning in her ear.

Every colour of arousal known to women blazed through her cellulite thighs. Before he changed his mind, she skated her fingers along his chest and looped her fingers around his neck chain from the opening in his shirt. Burned from the touch however, she hauled away her hands and shook her head.

"Not now," she whimpered, changing her mind.

A low chuckle cracked from his lips.

"Thought I'd pay you a hush visit and ask you to lunch. From what I've seen, you've had a great day. Have lunch with me, babe."

Her heart almost pushed out of her chest.

"OK."

She played it cool as if deliciously handsome men asked her to lunch every day. When in fact, she could not remember the last time a guy she dated showed up where she worked and asked her to have a meal with him. Never was more like it.

"How long do you need?" His deep voice made everything so much more exciting.

"Five minutes. Let me pack up and have a word with my boss. Then I'll be yours for an hour. Cool?"

He appraised her from head to toe with his eyes. "Cool. Before you go—"

His hot gaze raised her heat level from zero to twenty. One gaze. No. One sexy hazel gaze.

Bowing quickly, he brushed his mouth across her nose before hosing her lips with his tongue.

A burst of passionate excitement lashed through her body. She clutched his shirt with both hands, pulled him nearer and dished her tongue along his bottom lip. He sharpened his kisses. Quivering on her feet, she stroked the inside of his mouth with her tongue. He tasted like the best wine in all of America and Europe.

About twenty-five minutes later, they were seated inside *Baci Restaurant* along *Morena Boulevard*, thirteen minutes' drive from her office.

While she sipped club soda with a splash of cranberry juice and, Ryder descended on his club soda with bitters and lime in the opulent dining area, one black-tie waiter who had taken their order earlier delivered their hors d'oeuvre, two plates of *antipasti*. The range of cured meats, olives, heirloom tomato, basil, pepperoncini, mushrooms, fresh mozzarella, pickled meats, and vegetables in extra virgin olive oil served on an oblong platter made her stomach gripe.

By the time her second course, swordfish *oreganato*–a breadcrumb encrusted swordfish baked with white wine and garlic–was placed in front of her, she tried not to feel too guilty about the thirty-two-dollar cost of the dish. Well, she almost never had lunch at a fancy restaurant, so why deny her palate what she imagined would be a great meal?

Ryder did not blink at the thirty-four-dollar bill for his main of veal chop *lamberti* either. According to the waiter who served the dish, he explained that her boyfriend's main course was grilled tender veal chop topped with roasted garlic.

"Want to taste?" Ryder invited, after he handled his cutlery.

She could have sworn his eyes surged with desire. "If you're feeling generous, I'll taste."

He sliced the meat and pushed a small bite inside her mouth with his fork. She chewed slowly because she wanted to taste the flavours locked in the tender, moist juice.

"This is Italian fine dining," she murmured after she finished chewing. "Nice, thank you."

With every bite she ate, Kiarra wondered how her unsolicited visits to her neighbour's condo had now turned into a full-blown whirlwind romance.

Midway into their lunch date, she offered Ryder a piece of her breaded swordfish. He accepted the piece and winked as he chewed.

"I might try that next time," he thought out loud.

"Next time?"

"Yeah. This can't be our last lunch date, right?"

"Ow. Okay. Sounds perfect."

Why ever not? She would not overthink, or rationalize her relationship with Ryder. *Go with the flow,* she told herself. A man who did not worry about paying bills was surely God sent.

"It was finger-licking delish!" she voiced out after they were done eating their main.

"Yeah! Italian food cooked by Italian chefs served by waiters in tuxedos in a tucked away location. That's why I picked this spot."

"Relaxing atmosphere as well. I like it. Have you been here before?"

"Yeah, once with a client."

She was pleased he had not dined there with another woman on a date. It would have left a sour taste in her mouth. That would have been a shame considering how palatable her meal had been.

After eating their dessert, they stared at each other across the table wearing goofy smiles.

Maintaining eye contact, Ryder leaned forward. "You asked me a question on our trip to LA. I want to answer it now."

She sipped her drink. Ryder took her by surprise yet again. He had said during their helicopter ride that he would tell her about why he preferred a booty call as a way to escape an emotional relationship. But she had not expected him to raise the topic again. Another guy would have pretended he had forgotten the question she asked.

Folding her hands on the table, she nodded.

"Go ahead. I'm listening."

His face then hardened into a block of ice. He averted his gaze and stared out of the window. "Where do I start? This is hard," he said, his tone icy.

"Look at me, Ryder." When he did, she lifted one brow. "Don't say anything if you're not ready."

"Okay. Let me cut it short. I can't do the whole bare-your-soul thing."

She shrugged. "Go on. Whatever it is, I'm not going anywhere."

He grinned, but it was a grin cut from glass.

"I've got commitment issues." He hesitated.

Instead of speaking to fill the silence, she sipped from her drink while she waited for him to continue.

"It was easier for me to run away from a serious relationship by calling up someone who wouldn't demand for more after sex. It was my way of life, but it didn't take away the numb and empty feeling inside. I was lonely."

Winking, she nodded. "I noticed."

He chuckled, but it sounded crackly. "Why did you want to save me? I didn't make it easy on you."

"Oh, you made my life a living hell, trust me. I reported you to my friend, Taleisha a few times."

"What did she say?" His eyes flecked with regret.

"She said to stay away from you for my own good."

"But you didn't listen. Why?"

"Because I couldn't." Giving a slow shrug, she shook her head. "I'd never prepared meals for a guy before. I just saw myself doing stuff for you I've never done for any guy. Trust me, I wanted to stop."

"What was it that made you keep coming back?"

"I saw things in your eyes you didn't say. Even when you lashed out at me, your eyes kind of begged me not to give up on you. It was the way your eyes switched colours. I knew you wanted me to stay and to be there for you even though your mouth said I should leave and not come back. I couldn't explain it."

Her boyfriend moved his hand along the table and clasped it over her forearm. Wonderful warmth peppered her skin, scalding her in unhurried coils.

"I'm happy you got the message from God knows where. Every time you left after staying with me for hours, I felt like a scumbag. I hated myself for lashing out. I didn't believe you wanted me for me. I didn't like myself much, so I didn't see what you wanted from me, or what you saw in me. Yet, I felt a kick in my stomach once the key turned in the lock. Each time I saw your face, I felt this rush of odd emotions. I wanted to hug you. Then I'd tell myself you're too good for me and I'll start the hate all over again."

Smiling she peered into his eyes. Joy burst free inside her chest. The thrill descended to her belly.

"What a struggle on both sides. When did you decide you wanted to date me, Ryder?"

"When you made me blueberry pancakes, I knew you were special. No one had made me pancakes since my mom. It was a big moment for me. But then you didn't come back after that."

"Yeah. I decided to listen to what you said. Did you miss me then?"

"I think I'd a panic attack off and on for six days."

She blinked. "*Panic attack*? Are you serious?"

"Guess I didn't know what I had until you turned off from me. I decided to return the favour and show up at your place without notice. Waiting for you to come home that evening was excruciating."

"Then I returned with Zack."

His fingers gripped her arm tighter before relaxing.

"Anyway, that's my reason."

"I see how you glossed over the actual reason you've got commitment issues. Want to talk about that?"

"Not sure. Want to talk about why you satisfied your urges with a friend-with-benefit alternative?"

The drink she had in her mouth nearly oozed out. She shoved her hand over her mouth to seal in the liquid before swallowing in haste.

He waggled his eyebrows. "What? You think I'm the only one who needs to come clean?"

Giggling, she shook her head. "I already did. And you only gave part of your back story anyway."

"It comes out in small doses. Your turn, babe."

Feeling cornered, she exhaled. To gather her thoughts, she wanted to push back from the table. But Ryder's hand restrained her escape. So, she lifted her eyes to his own.

"Talk to me, Kia."

She blew out air in a slow cycle. "Kia?"

"Do you like pet names?"

"Oh yeah," she nodded, laughing and trying to ignore his steady caresses. You call me, babe already."

"Then Kia it is from now on along with babe."

"Okay. Both sounds fabulous to me."

"I'm eager to hear your back story, Kia."

From her inside the bud flowered and a smile bloomed on her cheeks. Inhaling fast, she started.

"Well, it was a great way to cope after a particularly dark time in my life. I'd a nasty break up and a big loss." Out of nowhere she felt her eyes water and she knew it was time to apply the brakes. "I can't do this."

Ryder pulled her to her feet, came around the table and dragged her into a warm embrace. Mindful of her makeup though, she tried not to stain his sparkling white shirt. When she sniffed, he offered her his pocket square. After she wiped her nose, she realized the fabric was silk. *Hmm.* Luxury day wear.

Inclining his head, Ryder draped his mouth over hers right by the window inside the restaurant. He did not care that people within and outside stared.

"Forget I asked, Kia. We'll talk about it when you're ready. I, more than anyone else knows how hard it can be to find the words to say what needs to be said."

Comforted he understood her hesitancy and unsaid pain, she nodded. "Thank you."

"Second dessert?"

"Yes please."

"Let's switch to a more relaxing spot."

Thoughtful and sensitive, he led her outside to the breezy patio. After he made sure she sat down without tears in her eyes, he kissed her forehead and dropped on the chair in front of hers across the circular table covered in white linen.

"Did I tell you I was awestruck by your outfit, Ryder? When you stood by the door in the conference room, I was like wow! Is this what you wear to work?"

Bending his head, he scanned his clothes before giving her a casual shrug.

"Had to see a client. I dress to please."

"Did it work?"

"Yeah. He's going to stock *Rich Earth Coffee* in all one hundred of his cafés around the country."

"Congratulations Ryder Blade! That calls for a celebration tonight. My treat."

"Great. I also want to take you out tomorrow to celebrate you signing new foster families."

She smiled. "Ow. So, it's got nothing to do with the fact you find me attractive, huh?"

Grinning, he caressed the side of her face and fanned her awareness with his admiring stare.

"That too, of course."

Nodding, she dunked her lashes and lifted her eyes to connect with his appreciative pair in a way she hoped told him how she felt.

"Where are we going tomorrow, July 4th, my Independence baby?" Going out on a date with Ryder was something she looked forward to with longing.

"Wait, to celebrate July 4th, do you usually hang out the American flag outside your home, and have fireworks exploding, accompanied with your local community band playing patriotic music?"

As he spoke, she nodded with vigour, smiling.

"Of course! Every year in Detroit, it was a big deal. Not much of fireworks though. We also had family barbecues going on, lots of chatter and laughter, eating and drinking. What about you?"

"Same thing, we had picnics with lots of fireworks."

"Nice. So, we're going where exactly tomorrow?"

"Out to the sea," he mooted with a cute grin. "We leave at ten in the morning. I want to treat you like you deserve to be treated. Like my queen. Besides, you left me with a rock-hard dick for days in that red dress you wore for our LA date."

Kiarra giggled so loud everyone on the patio swung their heads in their direction. The image of a naked Ryder doing his thing in his bathroom, or wherever kept her laughing a while.

Winking, he patted her hand. "Never heard me talk dirty?"

"This isn't the place, Ryder. How did you take care of your business?" She wiggled her eyebrows.

"Just know I didn't call any woman."

When she pressed her lips together, he grinned.

"I'd a cold shower. Did I stir a hot dance between your rounded thighs that night?"

Instantly aroused, she pinned her thighs together. Her nipples ached, beaded and skimmed her bra. Licking her lips, she whispered.

"With a chiselled body like yours and a charm that breaks down my walls, what do you think?" Her heart skipped as she told him the truth.

Their lunch date had turned out to be the best part of her day. No, her week. Best part of her year even.

His eyes dimmed, as he sucked in his breath.

"I want to hear you say it, babe."

"I was wet that night and every night I've been with you, Ryder. And now, I'm dripping on to my thongs."

Chapter 9 – What The Freak

Ryder

"**Hey** Jerrad!" Ryder grunted, clamping his friend's shoulder once they met up at the bar later on Friday evening.

"What's going on with Kiarra. Still unsettling you?"

"She's no longer a bother, bro."

"Meaning what?"

"Meaning I've had a change of heart. We're dating."

Jerrad's gaze zeroed in on, Ryder. "Are you sure this is what you want? You were very clear you didn't want anything to do with her."

"Things change, Jerrad. What can I say? Kiarra grew on me. Now I want to see where it goes."

"How long do you think this will last?"

"Look, I don't know. But I want to take deliberate steps to change my lifestyle."

Around them people chatted, laughed and ordered drinks.

Ryder ordered one round of dirty martini for two.

Jerrad frowned, his eyes puzzled. "What happened to booty call being the answer to our sexual needs?"

"I grew up, I guess. And you? Who was in your bed last night?"

Jerrad sipped his clear liquid. "I didn't ask her name."

"Drunken night?"

"Nah. But it was a pleasurable one." A self-satisfied grin appeared on his friend's thin lips.

Ryder discarded the lemon twist on his cocktail glass before taking a small sip from his drink.

"Maybe it's time to quit that lifestyle, J."

"Because Kiarra came crashing into your life?" his friend scoffed. "That's not going to last."

"Look, she's who I've been missing the whole time."

"What? You want to stay stuck to one woman?"

A shrug and a grin later, Ryder nodded. "I enjoy her company. I can't say the same for the other women."

"You think you'll feel this way in three months?"

"Don't know. I sure want to find out. Don't you want to find someone? You know, someone you find interesting? We're getting a little old for booty calls."

"I felt great until you threw a dampener on my experience. Now you're making me feel like crap for not asking her name last night."

"Let me tell you something, J. Before I met Kiarra, I was all gloomy and twisted with my dark thoughts. The day before she entered my condo, I'd a dream."

"About Kiarra?" Jerrad sneered.

"No point talking. You won't believe me anyway."

"I don't believe in dreams, bro."

"Just saying, I'm done with booty calls. I feel like crap afterward anyway. It's not a loss for me. There's something pure, intense and sweet about my relationship with Kiarra. Try it sometime."

"With Kiarra?" his friend teased.

"Yeah! And I'll kill you for real if you go near Kiarra, or even call her name twice."

Both men laughed.

"Find a woman who you find interesting, J."

"Is Kiarra the one then?"

Ryder shrugged. "That remains to be seen. I'm still exploring what we've got. You never know."

"Working with women who want fake boobs and butt doesn't exactly make it easy to find inspiring women with real hearts. All I've got are crumbs."

"Maybe I'll introduce you to Madison. She lives in one of our condos. Kiarra's friends with her."

"Is she a cantaloupe, or a grape? Don't say lemons!"

Jerrad laughed, so Ryder punched him on the arm.

"Sorry, I didn't check her boob size."

"Well, check first before undertaking to set us up."

"The only boobs I'm interested in belongs to my babe. Figure the rest out after I introduce you."

"Cantaloupe is what I go for, bro. Anything less, not interested."

"Not my problem. You can't break her heart. I don't want you putting my relationship with Kiarra in jeopardy." Ryder took another sip from his martini.

"We've come a long way, Ryder. If you find the one, I won't settle for crumbs. Set me up with Madison." Jerrad drank half his glass in one go.

"Will see what I can do."

"When do I get to meet your Kiarra?"

"Let me have a chat with her first. Will sort something out soon."

"Have you told her we're twin brothers from different moms?"

"Sorry. I forgot to mention that minor fact."

"You forgot? Have you told her about the–"

"No!" Ryder cut off his friend's question. "Don't mention it to her when you meet."

"If you want to get serious with this woman, you've got to share that with her."

"There'll be a time and place for that. It's all new. Let me enjoy the luxury ride."

"Your call. My advice? Don't leave it too late. Things like that have a way of blowing up in your face."

"I know that. In my own time, I'll tell her."

Kiarra

"Why didn't I hear about you dating, Ryder Blade until your tongue was found down his throat, hmm?" Taleisha complained the second, Kiarra opened the door to her persistent bell ringing the next day.

Laughing, Kiarra wiped water from her eyes.

"Girl, I was in the bath tub. I almost slipped trying to get out to open the door. Glad to see you."

"Why are you in the shower so early on Saturday morning?" her friend teased. "Going somewhere with your lover man?"

"Yeah. Going out with Ryder in two hours. Come into my bedroom. We've got a lot to catch up on."

"Wasn't Ryder in your office yesterday? He's taking you out again today? What's going on? Is he your boyfriend and no one told me? I need a drink."

Letting out a mock gasp, Taleisha marched to the kitchen, yanked the refrigerator door open and retrieved a bottle of red wine.

Amused at her friend's funny tirade, Kiarra walked backward to her bedroom.

"Bring your drink, meet me inside and I'll tell you everything."

"You better do."

Minutes later, Taleisha sat cross-legged on Kiarra's bed with a wineglass filled to the brim in her hand.

"My ears are itching. The last time we spoke, the guy couldn't stand your gut. What changed? I need to know how to get the guy I want. How did you move from enemies to lovers?"

Both women laughed so much, their eyes watered.

Kiarra did not stop moisturizing her legs even as she laughed. "We're not yet lovers. Ryder made me so mad, I boycotted his condo for a week. Then he came running after me, asking me to be his girlfriend."

Taleisha's eyes bulged as she choked. "Are you serious?" she asked after she swallowed. "How long did you do the chasing?"

"No kidding, girl. Up to three months. Every week I showed up, he gave me grief. I prayed so much for grace. I begged God to forgive me for never taking previous relationships seriously, for having sex before marriage. Ryder's rejection was hard to swallow. It stung. Just when I'd had enough of his rough side, he showed up in my condo one night. Zack and I found him waiting for me."

"Wait! He came in here with your key?"

"Nah! He made a spare key for himself."

Taleisha burst out laughing again. "Oh, so he used the same tactics as you. Karma!"

Giggling, Kiarra hooked her bra behind her back. "Yeah. I almost died of shock, honestly. I never thought he'd show up here."

"How did you feel?"

"Beyond excited. I was shaking inside. My stomach dropped out. My palms got sweaty in a split second."

"Oh gosh! Where you showing up in his condo because you were falling for him?"

"No! I'd no idea how the feelings crept up on me. I just knew I couldn't stop visiting him. I couldn't sleep well, or eat great."

Taleisha laughed non-stop. "How did Zack react?"

"He was as shocked as I was, girl. Ryder told Zack straight up he wanted me and he wasn't ready to share me with him."

"What the freak! Tell me, Zack went crazy?"

"Zack was surprised, but he didn't lose his cool. For that, I'm glad. I never talked to him about Ryder."

Eyes huge with shock, Taleisha took a long swallow from her drink. "You've got two guys on your ass, Kiarra. Are you saying I should give Jevonte space? Maybe I've been too forward with my feelings. I need a formula to capture that man."

They laughed hard while Kiarra pulled on a high-waist blue denim bum short. She twisted, pushed her head over her shoulder to stare at her butt in the dresser mirror.

"Wow! That shorts look hot on you, girl. What about the cellulite and stretch marks on your thighs? You could cover it up with full coverage foundation."

"No way. Every woman doesn't have cellulite-free thighs. Let Ryder see what I've got to offer and make his choice now before I fall head over heels in love and he tells me, I'm not a right fit for his super sexy ass!"

Quaking on the bed from laughter, Taleisha struggled to hold on to her half-full glass.

"I wish I was as confident as you. Rock it, girl!"

"Try it sometime."

"Maybe I should get bolder with my outfits. Jevonte might just take notice."

"I wore oversized t-shirts and jeans to Ryder's condo at the start because I didn't want him to think I was seducing him, or inviting him to pounce on me."

"Now I'm confused. Are you saying he found you attractive even in your oversized t-shirts and jeans?"

"Ryder said the day I made him blueberry pancakes he knew I was special. Can you believe that? Only God could have changed his mind."

"Only pancakes? Can't be that. Have you had sex?"

"No. But his kisses are sweeter than honey."

"Wow! Lucky you. God has heard your prayers, girl. Maybe I should go on my knees. Ending up alone isn't on my plan for my future. I need to stay warm at night. How can I get warm if I always sleep alone?"

"I'm with you on that one. Pray. If Jevonte's for you, he'll come find you."

Kiarra put on a white wrap top with crop sleeves. She tied the strings around her waist before applying primer on her face. Then she layered full coverage foundation on her face after concealing the few dark spots on her chin. When she finished her makeup, she wore a pair of white strappy wide feet wedges and grabbed her pre-packed beach bag.

"Wow! Where's he taking you for July 4th celeb?"

"Out to the sea, he said."

"That's romantic! When do I meet your boyfriend?"

Kiarra checked her watch.

"Calling him my boyfriend still sounds weird."

"Seriously?" Taleisha swallowed a gulp from her glass. "The guy buys you fifty roses infusing its exotic scent in your living room, wine and dine you and you need what else before you feel amazing enough to call him, your boyfriend?"

"I know. I'm taking it slow in my head, not in my heart. Ryder will be here soon. If you wait, you'll see him. Lock up when we're gone."

"Sure thing."

Kiarra sprayed two bottles of perfume, one after the other along her pulse points. "He got a good heart."

"Knock him out of his senses, girl."

Just as Taleisha set down her glass on the night stand, they heard the doorbell ping.

A jolt whipped through Kiarra's body as she darted toward the door. Taleisha was hot on her heels. When Kiarra opened the door, she hurried through with the introductions, eager to go on her date.

"Hey, Ryder, I want you to meet my best friend and partner in crime, Taleisha Hill."

Taleisha peered up at Ryder, smiling as she extended her hand. "Hi Ryder. Heard a lot about you."

Her date accepted the handshake but immediately removed his hand and placed it behind Kiarra's back.

"Nice to meet you, Taleisha. How are you doing?"

Taleisha skewed her head. "I'm good. And you?"

"I'm good. Looking forward to having a good time with my girlfriend."

Kiarra steered her gaze to her friend.

Both women exchanged knowing smiles.

"Don't break Kiarra's heart, Ryder. She's my bestie. I'll find you and make your life very miserable."

Ryder grinned. "Have no intention to do that."

"Okay. Have a nice time, you two."

"Thank you, girl." Kiarra followed her boyfriend out of her condo with her bag in hand.

Chapter 10 – Does Size Matter

Ryder

*O*ut on the Pacific Ocean moving toward *La Jolla Cove*, less than an hour later, Ryder laid next to Kiarra on the deck of his luxury yacht.

Lifting himself to rest on one elbow he shifted to gaze at her. Kiarra smiled. The morning rays bounced off her white teeth, enhancing her lustrous beauty.

"Kia, you look extra gorgeous today."

The denim shorts revealed her rounded thighs speckled with cellulite while her white wrap top tied tight around her waist emphasized her lovely boobs.

"Thank you, honey."

She coupled the endearment with a sweet wink that got his heart racing. It was too early to nurse a hard-on, so he opened a champagne bottle, one of the most expensive variants he had in his bar. A perfect blend of *Chardonnay*, *Pinot Noir* and *Pinot Meunier*. After he poured two flutes, he offered her one.

"Have a glass of champagne with me, my beautiful Kia. To current and future successes and to us!"

Smiling, she collected the flute and clinked it with his own. "To our future! Happy Independence Day!"

They each took long sips from their drink.

"Your bum short is the bomb! It cups your butt right and when you wiggle your butt as you walk, I find it very attractive."

She giggled, bending her head backward and her boobs jiggled on her chest.

By extension, his erection throbbed with longing.

"Hearing you say that makes me feel so good. I thought you'd be put off by the sight of my thighs."

"Why? Because of your cellulite, or stretch marks?"

"The cellulite mainly."

He gave a casual shrug before reaching out to caress her left thigh slowly. "Maybe if I was perfect myself, I'd be more critical. But I'm not. The cellulite is a flaw that adds spice to your beauty. I like it."

She laughed hard. "Never heard that before. But I'm good with it. Thank you. It means a lot. For the longest time, I thought their presence ruined my thighs and I tried to get rid of them. Over the last two years, my perspective changed. Now, I flaunt them."

"Flaunt it all for me. I could stare at you for hours, Kia. Your hips are deliciously wide and your boobs?" He angled his head. "You already know what I think." He sipped and watched her eyes sparkle more than their champagne drink. The woman he had come to respect shut her eyes as more giggles spilled out of her lips.

"My head is getting heavier with each compliment."

"That's a good thing. Your teeth are so white I can see myself in them."

Kiarra nudged him with her elbow. "My stomach hurts from laughing."

"But it's the truth. I'm not trying to get inside your pants, trust me."

"Whoa! OK. Would it be so bad if you were?"

Butterflies flew here and there inside his belly. He tossed his drink down his throat and set his glass down. So did his girlfriend. He slithered along the deck and laid closer to her. Turning to face her, he captured her hips with both hands. And she leaned forward, slung her arms around his neck and twisted one leg between his own.

For company, they had the silent blue sky, the rippling ocean water, the talking morning wind and the driver who understood his role–to be silent.

"When a man whose muscles vibrate against the fabric at his biceps, forearms, chest, abs, thighs says the nicest things to me, what do I do?"

Inching her head forward, she swept her tantalizing lips across his own in one wild caress that took him around the world. The awareness building up all morning erupted like a tornado between them. He squeezed her hips with his hands and showed her how he felt with his mouth and tongue. For many minutes, he excavated the juices out of her mouth and swallowed every drop with delight.

He was left in no doubt, Kiarra Wright was insanely attracted to him in much the same way he was to her. It felt awesome to find one woman he shared a mutual attraction with and also admired on many levels.

After she pulled back to catch her breath, he pinned slow kisses along her cheeks and temples.

"Did you always want to be a foster parent recruiter?" He breathed in her scent as he swallowed.

Lying back with one hand cushioning her head, she nodded. He braced himself with one arm, so he hovered over her to admire her features. Her hair packed into a bun and ponytail combo accentuated her high cheekbones. When she smiled, her face lit up in a way that made him feel like the luckiest man.

"Yeah. Back in Detroit, there were lots of kids whose parents couldn't care for them because of addiction, financial reasons and so on. They toured the streets, got lured into gang life and quite often, they needed to be loved and shown a different path."

"Like giving them a role model?"

"Oh yeah. Many of them had no dads. Their brothers and uncles were either in gangs, or in jail. The kids didn't know better."

For a brief moment, tightness formed in his gut. He forced himself to swallow. This was not the time.

"What's the success story of foster kids from your experience here in San Diego?"

"Many of them who give the system a chance and keep their heads down make it out in one piece. The teenage children are the worst hit. They rarely get adopted. They end up angry and bitter about life in general and then lash out. In the end, they've got to decide to turn their lives around, or stay in the rut."

He felt his heart rip at the corner for many reasons.

"Do the kids get therapy at all while in foster care?"

"Sure thing. And it helps them get past the rage and their underlying issues. Enough about what I do. You're everything a woman wants in a man, so how are you still single?"

Chuckling, he fell back on the deck. He shielded his eyes from the soft rays of the sun with his forearm.

"Why? Because I'm thirty-five this month?"

"Don't jump the question."

Sidling to his side, she coiled one hand around his chest, partly visible from his unbuttoned dark grey shirt. The comment she made to him at her office yesterday afternoon about wanting to touch his chest resonated in his head. With her eyes lowered, Kiarra played with the sprinkling of hair and his neck chain. He loved this territorial side she had unleashed on him. A woman who initiated kisses and was not afraid to show him she wanted him was both hot and sexy.

"In all sincerity, I haven't been looking for a wife."

"Why not?" She studied his face with curious eyes that appeared a golden brown under the sunlight.

"I wasn't ready emotionally."

"Are you emotionally ready now?"

"What?" He twisted his brows. "To get married?"

Kiarra pinched his nose and released it after he protested with his hands tickling her waist. She slumped on the deck, butt forward. He caught her with both hands and sat her upright.

"It's a process. I'm on my way there."

"What's hindering you from giving your all?"

"Coming from a broken home and seeing how marrying the wrong person can ruin many lives, I can say I was scared to my core for a long time."

"Makes sense. Do you remember our very first meeting when I asked if you'd marry me?" Her nose was a work of art, straight and long and beautiful.

He exhaled through his mouth, shaking his head. "Honestly, I thought you were nuts. It was one question I was running away from. And you asked in front of everyone like it was something of a joke."

She giggled. "So, you disliked me instantly?"

"Yeah. I thought, hey, stay away from the crazy."

Laughter bolted out of her lips, making everything around great. "But I wouldn't leave you alone, huh?"

He stroked her thigh with his middle finger and circled her knee.

"I'm pleased you stuck to me, Kia. Now, I'm the one who wants you around because I can't get enough of you. And I'm sticking to you the way you stuck to me."

They both burst out laughing for a while.

"If you were to sum up in two words what you wanted in a wife what would it be?"

"How does every conversation from your lips steer toward marriage?" It was one topic he avoided.

Shrugging, she tilted her head. "I find it interesting and I'm not shy to bring it up. I'm thirty-one in August. I want a family. I want to have kids and I want a husband who loves me as much as I love him. If that's not what you want in the near future, I'm wasting my time, don't you think?"

Bowing his head, he furrowed his brow. The thought of losing her made him nervous in every way. One thing was sure, he wanted her around now and, in the days, and months ahead.

"One thing I can say is that I want to be with you now and in the near future. Is that good enough?"

She beamed. His pulse tingled and he grinned.

"Yeah. That'll do for now."

"What's the stupidest thing you've ever done, Kia?"

Rubbing her finger against her nose, she paused.

"Once I went skinny dipping in a stranger's pool."

Shaking with mirth, he slapped the deck. His date hooted with him, covering her eyes with one hand.

"Did you get arrested for trespassing?"

"No. The owners weren't around, thank the Lord. The neighbour caught us and raised the alarm, so we jumped out of the pool, grabbed our clothes and made a run for it. We dressed on our way home."

He could not stop laughing as he imagined a naked Kiarra running for her life.

"Somehow I find it hard to imagine you would do something like that."

"Why do you say that? Teens do stupid things."

He nodded. If anyone knew that for sure, he did. "Agreed. But you seem so proper most of the time."

"Most of the time?" She arched her eyebrows.

"Sneaking into my condo with keys I didn't give you on many occasions remind me of you skinny dipping in a stranger's pool. You've got zero fear level."

Giggling, she shoved his chest with both hands. "Trust you to add it up to get a clean picture."

He grabbed her hands and pinned her to his frame. Slowly, he landed on his back on the deck with her. He clamped her butt with his palms and squeezed.

A razor-sharp jolt pricked his groin.

Kiarra gasped, pressing her breasts along his chest.

Lying thigh to thigh, he massaged her butt cheeks. Catching his face with both hands, she trapped his bottom lip with her tender lips. Ravenous for more, he explored her mouth. She tasted of the exotic sweetness of the champagne. He caressed the interior of her mouth a while before she pressed down on his chest with her palms and sat up on his thighs.

Thrilled he had her exclusive attention, he locked one hand behind his head and toured her waist exposed in the gap of her clothes with his right hand.

Giggling, she jiggled her butt across his thigh.

"You're tickling me," she whimpered. "What's the craziest thing you've done?"

"Your laughter is honied melody to my chest, Kia. Laugh some more." He carried on tickling her waist.

Kiarra laughed until she stopped him by gripping his hands. "Stop tickling me, Ryder. Please."

"Craziest thing?" He pushed back the worst page of his life before he said. "Printed my own dollar bills at *Denver Money Museum* and went to the candy store to try and spend it."

"Then what happened?"

"Got caught. The store owner called my parents."

"Wow! I bet your parents gave you a hard time."

"Sure. So, who did you go skinny dipping with?"

"My boyfriend at the time."

"Oh. Did you have sex in a stranger's pool?"

"No!" She shook her head. "That's not why we went there. We were adventurous and mischievous."

"Did you love him?"

"I was about seventeen." Her nose crinkled.

It was weird that he missed a chunk of his youth because he had been adventurous while she went on to have a great time.

Kissing her lips, he whispered. "Did you love him?"

"Why is that important? It was a long time ago."

"It's important to me." His chest tightened with jealousy, or something similar.

"Why?"

"Because I want to know more about you."

"Yeah. I did. He was my first."

Something inside him ripped to pieces. It was raw pain in his heart. Imagining his Kiarra being in love with the guy she gave her virginity simply rubbed him up the wrong way. But he shut out the thought.

"What about you? Have been in love before?"

It took several seconds for her question to register in his head. He blinked, gathering his thoughts.

"Once. We met at a sales conference in New York. We dated for two years."

"Why did it end?"

"We wanted different things." Although the reality was a little different, it did not matter because the relationship ended anyway.

"As a sales guy you could sell anything, how did you settle for coffee?"

He breathed a lot easier. "When I was growing up, my dad brought home two varieties of coffee beans from his travelling. Did my research by grinding a combination of the varieties. Made my own coffee pot, compared the aroma, taste and so on."

Kiarra drew long lines along his biceps and forearms, making it tough to assemble his words.

"How old were you?"

"Ten, or so. I just knew it was what I wanted to do."

"So, do you feel fulfilled in your role in sales?"

For the life of him, he did not know how to answer.

"It's rewarding in many ways, I tell you. And you? Is recruiting foster parents and homes everything you hoped it would be?"

"Every day comes with a host of different challenges that keeps me on my toes. The reward comes when kids either get adopted, or when they find love and safety in foster homes."

He lifted her leg and placed it on top of his own. Feeling her supple skin against his was perfect.

"Have you ever dated a black woman?"

Scrolling his fingers along her thick, sun-loving legs, he shook his head. "Not to my knowledge."

His girlfriend hooted, bumping her other leg against his feet as she rolled.

"Have you dated a white guy before?"

"If you count Zack, then yes, once."

"You didn't have an emotional connection with him, so for me that doesn't count."

She doubled over, as laughter rocked her body. He felt good watching her face sparkle.

"If it makes you feel better, that's fine," she agreed.

Caging her chin with one hand, he pulled her face closer. "Yeah, it does. When you laugh, the sound is like the best music I've ever heard and your face just brightens up everything around you." He stroked her lips with his tongue before he let go.

Kiarra pushed forward and followed his lips with hers. Finding her utterly alluring, he plugged her mouth with his tongue and for as long as possible they kissed. When they pulled apart, her eyes smouldered. And his body pulsed with deep heat that filtered into his bones.

"Fast forward to months ahead," she started moments later. "Will your family have a problem with you dating me, Ryder?"

"I don't think so. Not that it matters to me. The only person whose opinion matters is my sister's, Alana."

"Tell me about, Alana."

"At thirty-two, Alana's married to Alex. He's a good guy, a former pro basketballer turned fitness coach. No kids yet. As a sales ambassador, Alana loves her life in Las Vegas."

"You mentioned that previously. Everyone in your family's into sales, except your mom. Interesting."

"True. kind of runs in our blood. What's your best food to cook, babe?"

"Baked ziti."

"What's that?"

"You never had some?"

"Nope. Never even heard of it."

"Oh, you're missing good food, Ryder. It's baked macaroni, ground beef, tomato sauce and cheese."

"Going to cook me ziti sometime then?"

"We'll see. I make mine spicy."

"That's not the answer I was hoping for. I've been trying out new recipes I got online. Nothing spicy yet. For now, we're at *La Point Jolla* and we're going snorkelling at *La Jolla Cove*. Ready?"

It was only then she looked around. Her eyes went round and large on her face. "Snorkelling? Really?"

He fully unbuttoned his shirt and pulled off his shorts and loafers. "Yeah. There's a *24-hour Shark Snorkel Tour* in *La Jolla*. Done this before?"

"No. But I know how snorkel works. Don't try to breathe with your nose, or else the mask will quickly fog up," she recited. "Sharks? That's scary."

"You've got it. Only breathe through your mouth in relaxed, normal breaths. Don't worry about the sharks. It's the harmless leopard sharks. That's safe."

"Yeah. Got it."

After she stripped off her bum short and top, his heart jerked up at triple rate. *Damn!* Her white bikini was a gem on her body. Okay, her full-figure was not firm, but the woman had a sex appeal rating that blew his mind and gave him a thumping hard-on.

"Let's suit up, or you want to swim in your bikini?"

"Wetsuit preferably."

Excluding her belly, Kiarra had a groin-tightening butt and lush boobs that made his pulse do a backflip.

They put on wetsuits, swim fins, diving masks and snorkels. Once they were suited, he held her hand, gave a nod and they dived straight into the cool waters. Together they swam through the Pacific

Ocean, alongside interesting fish of diverse colours, giant turtles, harbour seals, sea lions until they reached the stunning flora surrounded by white sand bed. Smiling, they wandered around the astounding scenery for about eight minutes before they swam back to the surface.

Back up on the deck, they peeled off their gear.

"Did you enjoy being underwater, babe?"

"That was awesome!"

She shook water from her hair and let down her ponytail. With water dripping from her skin, she was the perfect picture of arousal. To clear his thoughts, he guided Kiarra down the stairs to the main cabin.

"I truly loved it underwater, honey. Snorkelling with you was a beautiful thing," she told him, smiling.

His body charged with happiness and current, he could not speak, so he nodded instead.

"Born to dive and swim, you were magnificent."

"You think so?" He finally found his tongue.

"Of course. You're a natural. I just did whatever I saw you doing."

They laughed.

"Babe, I'm happy you enjoyed being with me."

"There's nowhere I'd rather be on July 4th."

Claiming her face with one hand, he smooched her lips before saying, "I'll go get you a robe and a towel."

When he returned from the storage cupboards, he held the towelling robe behind her. Of course, it gave him a chance to spy her butt one more time. She shrugged her hands into the sleeves and belted it.

"Thank you," she murmured.

Reaching forward, she kissed his lips before he led her by hand to the galley kitchen.

"There's food over here," he told her with a grin.

"Cool." A huge smile coloured her face. Chicken salad with avocado and cheese. I love it!"

"With ribs and rib eye steak," he pointed out.

Nodding, she eyed the array of food on the table while he poured two glasses of white wine.

"And mashed potatoes, corn bread and corn on the cob. That's very thoughtful of you, Ryder."

"I see you approve. We've worked up an appetite. Time to have fun filling up the tank."

She laughed. "That's right. I approve."

While they feasted, she slanted her head and her dark brown eyes gleamed with mischief. "I want to ask an awkward question. Do you mind?"

He chuckled, raising his glass. "Might as well."

"What kind of women did you date in the past?"

"Don't go there, Kia."

"Seriously. I'm not going to be offended, I promise. I just want to know the good, the bad and the awkward about you. Note, I didn't say the ugly."

"Trust me, like everyone else, I've got an ugly side."

"OK. We'll get to the ugly side sometime."

Though he knew she was right, her statement unnerved him. He scratched his head and tuned his thoughts to the question on the table.

"Slender blondes mainly."

"Like Hailey."

He shrugged. "You could say that."

"So why me now?"

"Because you're unique. I've never even dated a brunette. Everything about you is different."

She raised one eyebrow. "Are you serious?"

"In every way, you're my first and I love that about you, about what we share. It's refreshing."

"Great answer."

After they finished eating, they put on their own clothes and he joined her on the couch.

"It's my turn to ask an awkward question."

Shaking her head, Kiarra burst out laughing.

Hiding his grin, he asked. "Why are you laughing?"

"I'm sure you're going to shock me."

"Maybe. My question is, does size matter?"

At first, she squinted, then she started to giggle. "What size are we talking about?"

"Mine for a start."

"Why? Is it small?"

Laughter exploded through him. He fell back on the sofa as he quaked.

"No. I'm not small down there."

"Phew! That's a relief."

"You haven't answered my question."

"Ah, yes, size matters, come on, Ryder. Where's the satisfaction if it's small?"

"Just asking. I'm curious, that's all."

"And for you? Does size matter?"

To answer her question, he zeroed his gaze on her cleavage and edged to her side.

"Not really. But I'm delighted you've got boobs and butt I find extremely sexy."

Just as she opened her mouth, he grabbed her shoulders, lifted her to her feet and cuddled her.

Music floated inside the boat and gushed out to the sea. He powered his hands across her back and butt, breathing in her ocean scent with delight. "Look out of the window." On cue, fireworks exploded in the distance in a mixture of red, blue and white colours.

Kiarra squealed, whimpered and moulded his body with hers while her hands paraded up and down his back. "It's beautiful!"

Stirred from head to toe, he dipped his head and silenced her soft moans with his mouth.

Chapter 11 – Who Is She

Kiarra

"*Tell* me what's going on in your head right now?" Kiarra queried, licking her lips.

It was Saturday afternoon, on her boyfriend's birthday and she was lying on his sofa with her head crouched on Ryder's thigh.

In the last week, Ryder had begged her not to do anything for his special day except to spend the day with him in his condo. So, she had worn a fitting outfit in the form of a glitter black and gold bodycon dress, got him two gifts; a grey personalized robe he decided to wear over his shorts and shirt because he loved it and, a personalized chopping board, he promised to put to frequent use.

Ryder traced his fingers along her face.

They just finished eating slices from his birthday cake. That was after they had feasted on the Thai food, he insisted she ordered from *Amarin Thai Cuisine*. Their feast of beef curry, fried shrimp wrap, basil fried rice, noodles with duck and a whole fried fish accompanied with three sauces was terrific.

Caressing her hairline with the pad of his fingers, his eyes narrowed as he spoke.

"Still wrestling with the fact that I'll open my eyes someday and this will all have been a dream."

Curving a little to face him, she caught his muscular shoulder with her right hand.

"Hey! Don't say that. I know this all seems too good to be true for both of us, but we've got to believe this is real for it to work."

"Do you believe in us?"

His eyes switched to a green hue. In the pair, she read uncertainty. So, she wrapped her palm along his angled jaw, petting the sculpted line with her fingers.

"Look, you've got me in your arms. We're exclusive. What can go wrong?"

He chuckled. "A lot."

Squinting, she tried to figure out what exactly was going through his head. "Like what? Help me out. It's your birthday, honey. Forget every dark thought."

"If I knew why I wouldn't be wrestling in my mind."

"In my book, that means, forget it and kiss me."

Grinning in her face, he buffed her back with his right hand, steadied her neck with his left and branded her lips with his own.

"Now tell me, what's the biggest decision you've ever made?" The thought just occurred to her and she was a little curious.

His face closed up. The harsh jawlines reminded her of his signature scowl when he first moved in.

"Ah-ah. Don't do that." She grasped his jaw and tapped his chin. "Talk to me, Ryder."

Blinking, he relaxed. "Cutting my parents out of my life. Before you ask, it was the best thing for me."

For a tiny moment, she shut her eyes. Inhaling deeply, she opened her eyes and stared at him.

"Do you regret it?"

"No. It was long overdue."

"Was your relationship with them that bad?"

Her response was cut off by a rap on the door followed by the doorbell.

"Expecting someone?" she asked, eyeballing him.

Shaking his head, he lifted her off his thighs and sat her on the sofa. Grinning, he bent his head and kissed her lips before straightening.

"Be back. Don't go anywhere, Kia."

Blowing him a kiss, she whispered. "I've not got magic powers."

Responding with a snicker, he hurried along. "Are you sure about that?"

"Sure, honey."

When he turned to the hallway, she crossed her legs, still feeling relaxed. She touched her fingers to her mouth, newly-kissed by her gorgeous boyfriend's cute lips. Ryder Blade was a great kisser every time.

Next thing, Kiarra heard argument from the doorway. She swept down her legs and hurried toward the front door. Who was he fighting with out there?

"You're not welcome here," Ryder was saying.

"Just listen to me, Ryder," a white older woman pleaded, evidently not taking his word to heart. "It's your birthday and I've come to spend time with you."

"You stopped listening to me a long time ago. I've got a guest. Please go back to wherever it is you came from. I'm not available, or interested."

"Hear me out," the woman who stood with her head reaching his shoulders insisted.

With Ryder blocking her view, Kiarra could not see the woman's face.

"No!" His tone was curt and severe.

After listening to their back and forth squabble and hesitating for a while, Kiarra spoke up. "Ryder?"

"I'll be right there. She's leaving," he told her.

Twisting his neck to the side, he threw her a don't-get-involved stare.

"Not if you don't listen to me," the chestnut-haired woman at the door insisted. Her semi-full lips were now pinched at the corners. Attired in an expensive-looking sky-blue suit and nude heels, the nude handbag on her arm suggested designer quality.

"Who's she?" Kiarra asked, not moving from her spot by the start of the hallway.

"I'm his mom," the woman supplied, her hazel gaze pleaded for her understanding.

Hmm. Ryder had his mom's eyes and long nose.

"Go back to your fancy hotel," Ryder maintained.

"Let your mom come inside, Ryder. Please. Today is your birthday."

It was the right thing to do as far as Kiarra was concerned. She had no idea why he told her earlier he had cut off his parents from his life. But if his mom showed up on his doorstep begging, he could at least open the door for her.

Ryder stood back to allow, Kiarra get past him to greet his mom at the door.

"Thank you. I'm Lindsay Blade. And you are?"

"Hello Mrs. Blade. My name's Kiarra Wright. Please come inside, ma'am."

Lindsay stared at her son for access. "Move. Your friend says I can go inside."

With his expression still grim, Ryder stood there blocking the entry.

"Can't let you inside. You left me a long time ago. Go save the precious lives that matter to you," her boyfriend insisted, not shifting ground.

Kiarra stared up at Ryder and placed one palm on his chest. She moved her hand up and down.

"Go inside and have an adult discussion with your mom. Can you do that for me?"

"There's nothing more to be said." Ryder's eyes darkened and his words were as hard as granite.

"There's more, Ryder. If you don't allow her inside, I'll go to my condo. Don't bother to come find me."

His eyes widened in shock perhaps. "What are you saying, Kia?"

"Listen to your mom. Can you do that, for me?"

Giving him an ultimatum was not her favourite thing but she could not stand by and watch him disrespect the woman who gave birth to him.

Ryder stepped back and marched toward the living room. Anger rolled off his broad shoulders and his face was as gloomy as a blustery night.

Lindsay mouthed a grateful, "Thank you," as she entered with cautious steps.

"You're welcome," Kiarra mouthed back. "Has he always been this grumpy?" she side-whispered.

"No." Solemn-faced again, Lindsay shook her hair tied in a semi-neat bun that looked like she woke up with the hair in place. But in truth, it probably took over an hour to achieve the style.

Once they all stood in the living room, Ryder sat up straight-back on the single-arm sofa nearest to the kitchen as if he needed to be far away from Lindsay.

"Please sit down, Mrs. Blade," Kiarra said after a lengthy awkward pause stretched without Ryder offering his mom a seat.

"Thank you, Kiarra. Do you live here with my son as well? It's a lovely space."

"Our living arrangement has nothing to do with you," Ryder dived in, cutting off the need for Kiarra to respond. "What do you want?"

Whatever happened between these two, must have played a role in shaping her boyfriend to become the gloomy, cold adult she had known for the first few months. Ryder was relentlessly harsh when he tried.

"A relationship, Ryder. Happy Birthday," his mom replied after she sat opposite him on another single-arm sofa. "I have come all this way so we can start to build a relationship again."

"Now you've got ample time to build a relationship with me?" Ryder scorned, glowering at his mom. "Where were you when I was in third, fourth, five grades, up to my senior year? Where were you when I needed you to show up for my games, school plays, spelling contests and school fund raising events?"

It was the first time she had heard him speak with the desperate need of the child deprived of parental love. The brokenness he exuded broke Kiarra's heart. Her eyes pooled with tears. She hated to hear him sound, so bitter and cracked. Should she go to him? Not sure what to do, she remained seated on the kitchen seat and wiped her eyes with her fingers.

Lindsay sighed. "I know I could never give you back what you're asking of me–"

"Asking of you?" Ryder interrupted, his tone dead-cold. "I'm not asking anything of you, ever."

"Give me a spot in your life. I did a lot of good in the world because it was what I was put on earth to do."

"That's it! You can never take responsibility for your inactions. It's never your fault. You were put on this earth to be a mom first!" he barked.

Lindsay nodded and lifted one hand.

"I'm not done. The moment you had kids, you became a mom, not just a surgeon. And you failed!"

His sharp words cut through, Lindsay's denial.

"It wasn't easy for me to miss out on my kids' lives. I gave up on the most important people in my life. Do you think I don't know that?"

"Pathetic! You just realized that at sixty-five? As a child when I asked for your help to do my homework, you told me you needed to go save lives of those who depended on your expertise."

"I'd very sick people who needed brain surgery, Ryder. Are you going to hold that against me all the days of my life?"

"That's my point. I don't need you now. I don't need your affirmation about anything. You taught me to be independent, not to rely on you for anything I needed emotionally. You abandoned me and Alana. So, go to your patients who need surgical help and leave me the hell alone! End of discussion."

Ryder jumped off his seat and marched to the bar. He poured himself a drink and took a long gulp.

"But you never lacked anything money could buy."

"The show is over, Lindsay Blade. Go home."

The scene reminded Kiarra of their shaky start.

"I'm sorry I can't give you back the years you talk about. Let me start to make amends, Ryder. Please."

"Ever heard of a little too late? I'll cut you a cheque monthly. That's my final offer. Just leave me alone."

"That's not why I came here," Lindsay insisted.

"What happened to you? Are you sick? Or did they fire you? Are you retiring? Is this what this charade is about? You want me to believe you suddenly woke up to the reality your kids aren't in your life? That's the biggest joke of the century."

"Ryder, watch your tone. I'm still your mom."

Even though she was mad at her son for disrespecting her, Lindsay uttered the rebuke without a thread of anger. Kiarra knew exactly what her own mom would have done if she dared spoke out of turn. White folks got away with blue murder with their parents.

"Mom?" Ryder jeered. "What will you do if I don't watch my tone? You'll leave here and go to your beloved patients? By all means, go. No one is stopping you."

After a long pause, Lindsay carried on. "I'm not sick. Retirement is staring me in the face, that's true."

"Then, it's your time to learn to live without me like I did without you. I adapted to your absence a long time ago, now there's no room in my life for you. Not even a tiny space. Do you get that?"

"What can I do to earn your friendship, Ryder?"

"Go back to your husband. That's where you should start. He probably needs you. I don't."

"Your father and I, are working on our relationship. But you and your sister also matter to me, to us."

Ryder clapped, his grin cynical. "Good for you. The way you see it, everything you want will fall into place when you want it and life returns to normal, right?"

"No. I've also suffered. I sacrificed my family for my career because it was one thing, I was good at."

"Most people do both!" Ryder yelled. "Why couldn't you? Why did you have to give us up, your kids?"

Kiarra ground her teeth to stop from flinching. It was getting harder to stay silent. Really hard.

This was one fight she did not want to meddle in.

Looking exasperated, Lindsay got on her feet and paced the room with her arms cuddling her body.

"I've been trying to reach you for over two years, Ryder. Two years. You've been pushing me away. I went to your mansion at Oceanfront Walk, you weren't there. As CEO of *Rich Earth Coffee*, do you think you can get away with hiding–"

Wait! Who's CEO of *Rich Earth Coffee*? Ryder? No! He's not CEO of anything. What did he say he did again? Sales Manager, that's right, Kiarra recapped.

Ryder skewed his head in Kiarra's direction. Her puzzled gaze met his own piercing pair. He tore his head aside to meet his mom's confused gaze.

"Go home. Go to your fancy hotel, I don't care. Don't come back here. There's no place in my heart, or my life for you because you made your choice a long time ago. Stick with it."

He moved toward the front door.

Lindsay gathered her designer bag. "Thank you, Kiarra. I wish we'd met under a different setting."

"It was nice to meet you. Goodbye, Mrs. Blade."

Kiarra watched her boyfriend hold on to the door while he waited until his mom stepped outside before slamming it shut. When he returned to the living room, she fixed her eyes on his own.

"Do you have something you want to say to me, Ryder Blade?" She was fuming inside her chest.

"Not now, Kiarra."

"Not now? Your mom said you're the CEO–"

"I know what Lindsay said," he interrupted, his tone chilly like on a frosty winter morning.

"Don't interrupt me when I'm speaking, Ryder. It's rude. And stop slamming doors, it's childish."

Clearly, his mom had not taught him simple manners. She had spent the last hour listening to Ryder put his mom in her place. Interrupting, Lindsay was out of order in Kiarra's code of conduct.

Ryder glared at her as if she was out of her mind.

"You know what? You've had enough grief for one day. So have I." She slipped down from the seat and headed for the front door. Right now, she did not want to be with a guy with a temper so cold, he could freeze the sun.

"Kiarra?" he called out. "Don't go."

"No!" She swirled around. "You lied to me. You lied to me over and over about what you do for a living. That's wrong. I just asked you about it and you said, *not now* like you've got a right to hold out on explaining something so crucial to me. It's called trust. I don't know who you are, Ryder Blade. I don't want to see your lying face again."

"Kiarra!" he hurried after her. "I can explain."

"It's over!" She wrenched the door open and fled out of his condo.

Chapter 12 – I Was A Fool

Kiarra

"*He* lied to me, Zack!" Kiarra almost sobbed.

"About his career. Has he told you why he had to pretend to be a sales guy instead of the CEO?"

"No! Does it matter? If he lied about his career what else is he not telling me?"

"Okay. I might not be Ryder's biggest fan because he stole you from me but I know he cares a lot about you. I'll give that to him. The guy's a bigger romantic."

Gripping Zack's arm, she dipped her head to avoid others in the bar eavesdropping on their chat.

"Ryder's a jerk! Why else would he lie to me? I've known him for many months. We've dated for months. Not long enough to be honest, right?"

"Did he explain when you asked?"

"His reply was *not now*."

Zack sighed. "There are many reasons people feel the need to alter the truth. Didn't you say he had an unpleasant argument with his mom before you asked him about this lie?"

"Yes, but that has nothing to do with his lies."

"It might be the reason he wasn't in the mood to explain."

"He was deflecting. Same thing you're doing now. Why are you on his side anyway?" She had expected Zack to be more persuaded by her argument.

"No. I'm not deflecting. If you want me to resolve the issue between you and Ryder, I can't because I want you back in my life, Kiarra. So, you've come to the wrong person."

Yes, she knew it was a long shot but she had to talk to Zack about her broken heart, because she needed a guy's perspective.

Frustrated, she kissed her teeth. Then she realized Ryder disliked her doing it. Well, he was a liar.

"What are you talking about, Zack? We parted ways months ago but we're still friends. And friends are there for each other."

"This friend loves you. I was a fool not to say it once I knew how I felt. I wanted to give you time. I thought you loved me. Why did you pick, Ryder over me? I'm nice all the time. He's not. He's a bad boy who'll probably break your heart and I'll kill him of course."

She raised her hands and shook her head.

"No. Please don't complicate my life right now. I'm not in the right state of mind for your conversation."

"Precisely!" Zack's eyes shone with victory.

"What?"

"That's how Ryder must have felt when you asked him to face the truth. He had just had a show down with his mom and you wanted an explanation for why he lied to you. So, he said, *not now*. Get it?"

Shocked by how Zack switched up their discussion, she shook her head. "What are you saying?"

"Give the man a chance to explain his side. If you're still not satisfied, come back to me. I'll get an engagement ring ready for when you do."

She exhaled and clamped her fingers around her friend's wrist. "Don't make a joke out of this, Zack. I'd no idea you were in love with me until afterward."

Her relationship with Zack had been clear cut. Fuzzy feelings never kept her awake at night.

"Neither did I until it was too late. Hang on, how did you know anyway?"

"Ryder told me."

"What? Ryder told you I was in love with you?"

"Mm-hm. He read you like a book when I couldn't."

"I warned him not to hurt you. Here you are looking like a lost puppy. Should I go ahead to kill him?"

Though she wanted to laugh at Zack's poker face, her feelings were hurt and all over the place.

"Honestly, I don't want to listen to anymore lies. It hurts too much."

"Then take a break. We could go to Hawaii for the weekend. I get my friend-with-benefit back and you get your broken heart fixed. What do you say?"

"Things can't go back to the way they were, Zack. It doesn't work that way. Ryder means—"

He shut his ears with both hands. "Don't say it. I don't want to hear how much Ryder means to you."

"Should we head home then?" she suggested, tired from a very long day at work before their evening out.

"Or we could go the club."

"Not in the mood, Zack."

"You'll be once we hit the dance floor."

"Don't know."

They strode out of the bar still arguing about where to end the dying Friday night.

Ryder

*D*esperate and feeling caged, Ryder punched the bag with intense force repeatedly in his home gym. Chunks of sweat dropped from his face. Tears leaking out of his eyes, mixed with the stream of perspiration.

From the haze of his frustration however, he heard a banging sound. Standing still, he listened. The banging sound continued. He peeled off his boxing gloves, slapped it on to the hook on the wall. With his towel in hand, he headed toward the front door.

No one knew where to find him except his runaway girlfriend and Jerrad. But Kiarra never knocked. Not even the first time she showed up. His chest tightened with pain. She had abandoned him just as he had dreaded.

When the thwack grew louder, he tugged the knob and dragged the door open.

"What do you want?" he barked at the guest.

Lindsay Blade had her hand raised half way up to hit the door, her soft chin set in a stubborn slant.

"I came to see you, Ryder. And I'm not taking no for an answer this time."

Lindsay barged past his arm and marched inside, reminding him of Kiarra's feisty attitude. He missed his girlfriend so much. Now he wished he had taken his time to ask, Kiarra about all her hiding spots.

Shutting the door in a hurry, he marched behind the woman who abandoned him a long time ago.

"Where do you think you're going, Lindsay Blade? I'm busy."

"Busy working out in the gym!" She stopped and spun on her heel. "I was a shitty mom to you and your sister. You were right. I hate to admit it because I hate failing. But I failed you and Alana. I wasn't there when you needed me. I can admit it now. Please, please forgive me. It's too late to go back in time, I understand that but I want to be a part of your life going forward. If you say no, I'll stay here until you say, yes. The guilt is killing me."

His mom dumped her bag on the rug and sat on the sofa, the same one, Kiarra had stretched on while they chatted before Lindsay Blade came in and ruined everything. That was a week ago.

A whole freaking week!

"I'm not interested in your drama today. You ruined my childhood and my teenage years, that's all water under the bridge as they say. But the last time you came here, you also broke up my relationship with Kiarra. She dumped me, Mom. Kiarra abandoned me on my birthday because of you. We were having a wonderful time before you ruined it all."

He had no idea how pain suddenly multiplied in his heart. Before he could figure out why, tears exploded in his chest and gushed out of his eyes.

Warm hands immediately cuddled his forearms.

He stiffened. Frankly, he wanted to shake away his mom's hands, but he knew she needed him as much as he needed her. And for the first time in however long, he reached for his mom, pulled her into his arms and wept on her shoulder. It was not an all-out cry. Just a short sob to clear his head and chest. OK. He wept like a baby. Like a July baby that Kiarra said he was. When last did he cry? He could not remember.

For several minutes, he tried to pull himself together with his arms still wrapped around his mom's shoulders. She tightened her hands around his waist and kept silent. It was what he needed–the silence. When he had cleared his head, he pulled back.

Chuckling, he wiped his face with his towel.

"I'm sorry I ruined your outfit with my sweaty self, Mom."

It felt good to call Lindsay, *mom* again without bile rising in his gut. It felt very good.

Laughing softly, his mom waved one hand.

"Are you kidding me? I've been looking for you to ruin my clothes for years now. Don't apologize."

"Look, I forgive you, Mom. But I want Kiarra back. That's the only way this can work." He waved one hand between them. "Kiarra means the world to me. She was there when I was miserable and lonely."

"How did she cope with your gloominess?"

"I honestly don't know. The woman has a loving heart and a thick skin. Yet she abandoned me for not revealing the truth. I'm a little confused."

"Why didn't you tell her you were the CEO? Most men would start with that fact."

"I wasn't planning on sweeping her off her feet. I came here to be anonymous. She came on to me strong and when I fell for her, she dumped me."

"Okay. Nobody likes being lied to, Ryder."

"Technically, I didn't lie. It's my company–"

"Yes, you did. Own it. Take full responsibility. It's what you've been preaching." His mom winked.

Grinning, he slanted his head. "Fine. I lied to her."

"Good. It's been a week. Go get her before someone else sweeps her off her feet. Kiarra's a keeper."

Fear whipped him into shape. "If I knew where she was hiding do you think I wouldn't have found her?"

"Hmm. What about her close friends?"

"One thing I know for sure, Kiarra isn't in any condo in this building. The concierges are on my tab. None of them has sighted her in a week."

His mom nodded in approval.

"Smart move. Then reach out to any of her friends who live elsewhere. A broken-hearted woman will run to family. Do you know anything about her family?"

"Yes. She's got a brother in Atlanta and a sister in New Jersey. Her parents live in Detroit. I don't see how she can abandon her job and move across the country just to get away from me."

Grinning, his mom slanted her head.

"What's funny?"

"Are you in love with Kiarra?"

"No. I don't know."

He shrugged, surprised at the question.

"Yes, you are. Never seen you cry before. Not even when you were so mad at me, or your sister, or your dad. Not even when your dog ate your homework when you were in second grade and you had to stay up to redo the whole thing."

Snorting, he recalled getting worked up about his paper being ripped to shreds by his favourite pet, pesto. Those were the best memories. His dog slept on his bed, ate at his feet and was his trusted companion until it got too sick to be one. He shook his head.

"I remember."

"If she moved away so you can't find her, then she feels the same way."

He blinked. "How can you be sure?"

"If she was indifferent to you, she'll be in her condo right now. If she isn't, then she has strong feelings for you and they aren't going away. So, she isn't over you yet. Just think about one friend she has that could provide the perfect hideout for her. Think."

After a short pause, he spoke out loud. "When a woman's is upset, will she go back to her ex?"

"Oh, you mean like men who run back to their vomit in something called rebound sex?"

Cringing, he grimaced. "Mom?"

"Women move on from their past for good."

"What if it was an amicable separation?"

"Do you suspect, Kiarra went back to her ex?"

"That's not why I'm asking?"

The thought Kiarra could have gone back to Zack kept him awake at night.

"Why are you asking? In some cases, women might go back to their exes if they've got a good friendship."

Fear clipped his gut. "I'm going to take a shower. Make yourself pancakes and have a drink on me."

"That's not the only meal I know how to make now, Ryder. I've improved over the years."

"Good on you, Mom."

Grinning as he strode away with his towel boarding his neck, he did not look back.

Chapter 13 – I'm Not Done

Ryder

"*Where's* Kiarra?" Nicole asked. "She's making a habit of skipping barbecue nights."

"We've got no clue what Kiarra's up to now," Jamie replied swigging his beer as he gave Ryder the evil eye.

"What we know is before Ryder got his jaws on her mouth, Kiarra was the life of this party."

That was Duane, the dark guy who Ryder suspected wanted Kiarra for himself.

"Keep my name out of your mouth, Duane!" Ryder growled, not in the mood to tolerate bullshit.

"One day you two are hugging it out and wrapping your arms around each other and the next she's avoiding you? What's going on?" Jason teased.

"Mind your own damn business, Jason! It's a great quality in a man. Besides, don't you all have anything better to do than to push your noses in Kiarra's relationship?"

"Don't hurt, Kiarra," Monica warned in her soft voice. "She means the world to all of us."

Ryder lifted his hands and set his drink down with a thud. "I'm not going to hurt her, Monica." He backed away from the barbecue area and moved toward the blue and white building. Before he met Kiarra, he did not mind being perceived as a monster. Now? It hurt.

Pain banged on his chest like in a slaughter house. He rubbed both hands across his head. Then he exited the condo block and went on a walk. It had been a week since his fight with Kiarra. The woman shut him out of her life like he never existed. He did not think it was possible. Okay, he had been afraid this would happen. That he would wake up and she was just a dream. Kiarra was too good for him. He knew it.

His mom knew it too, that was why Lindsay had abandoned him to make his way in life without her. He rubbed his palms up and down his face until he calmed down. But he deserved a second chance with Kiarra. He had earned it.

Either Kiarra no longer lived in her condo, or she had skipped the city. Every time he let himself inside her place, she was not there.

Where the hell was Kiarra?

Did she have to leave him like the rest of them?

Again, he got out his cell phone and called her number. Before now, he had left over a dozen messages. She did not return his calls.

"Hey Kiarra. What the hell are you doing to me? I'm sorry. Please come back."

The voice message was self-explanatory. He was going out of his arrogant, dark mind.

Then, his mom's words burst through his confused fog with a mighty force. He recalled Kiarra had called her friend, Taleisha from his phone once. Eager to find the number, he scrolled through his phone log. There! He found the it and swiped right. While waiting for Taleisha to answer, he licked his tongue.

"Hello?" Kiarra's friend greeted, her tone hesitant.

"Hey, Taleisha."

"Yes. Who's this?"

Rubbing his nape, he puffed out air from his mouth.

"This is Ryder Blade, Kiarra's boyfriend."

"Oh hey, Ryder. What's up?"

"How are you doing, Taleisha?"

"I'm great, thanks. Is everything okay with you?"

"No. I'm trying to find Kiarra. Is she with you?"

After a short interlude, Taleisha cleared her throat. "We were together earlier. Isn't she home yet?"

Turning his wrist, he glared at his watch. "It's nearly midnight. No, she's not and I miss her terribly, Taleisha. Help me out. Is she with you?"

"Yes. But I didn't tell you," she whispered.

"Okay. Can you send text me your addr–"

A dinging sound filled Ryder's ear. He yanked the cell phone from his face and glowered at it. The call had ended abruptly. But his phone beeped almost immediately. Scrolling through, he saw a text.

After he read it, he laughed for the first time in a week as he rushed back inside his condo.

Ryder

An hour later, Ryder clutched a giant gift in one arm, and other wrapped gifts in the other hand as he stood waiting for Taleisha's apartment door to open. He counted to ten while he waited.

Moments later, the door opened.

Astonished, Ryder rocked back on his heels.

Robed in a white and gold dressing gown with a towel tied around her head, Kiarra looked amazing even with her jaw splitting open. It seemed he was the last person she had expected to see.

"What are you doing here?" his girlfriend asked after she recovered, her tone stern.

"Hey. I'm sorry, Kia. I messed up. Please."

Humility was best served hot, so he grovelled.

Kiarra blinked and stepped back.

"How did you find me? Who gave you this address?" Next, she called out. "Taleisha!"

"Kiarra listen, please," he begged. "I was wrong."

Taleisha popped her head behind Kiarra. A wide grin settled on her round face.

"Hello Ryder. Great to see you here."

Kiarra glared from Taleisha to Ryder. "What's going on? Were you two talking behind my back?"

Taleisha shook her head at first. "Not really. Why don't you come inside, Ryder?"

"Thank you." Gladly, he stepped inside before Kiarra thought of shutting the door in his face.

"Look, Kiarra. There's no point running away from Ryder. He wants to talk to you. I'll leave you two."

"Here you go." Ryder handed a wrapped box to Taleisha. "Please accept it."

Smiling, Taleisha gushed. "Oh, thank you, Ryder."

"If you wanted me out of your condo, all you'd to do was say so, not sneak behind my back, Taleisha."

Taleisha flung her arms around Kiarra's shoulders. "I don't want you out. But you're miserable, so is he. Give him a chance to explain, girl. I love you. Bye."

Kiarra elbowed her friend. "I hate you right now."

Laughing, Taleisha clutched her side.

"You'll love me later when he throws you across my bed and gives you a good time in makeup sex."

Kiarra's breath hitched. Her mouth stood ajar as her bulging eyes followed Taleisha out of the front door.

Snickering under his breath, Ryder tried not to laugh out loud, but he could not hold back as his brain exploded with images of a naked, Kiarra across his sheets. That would probably be the best day of his life.

"That's not funny!" Kiarra jeered, clicking her teeth.

Handing over the giant personalized teddy bear, he shook his head and cleared the fun from his face. Her teeth kissing that he disliked now sounded like music.

"Yeah, you're right. I came to apologize, babe."

Without hesitating, she reached for the golden-yellow teddy bear and stared at the round photo on its soft belly. It was a screenshot of the two of them on their date inside the helicopter several weeks ago.

A smile bloomed on her face. And his heart juddered. It even did a squishy dance of relief.

Then he handed her a wrapped box.

She accepted it, and turned to walk inside. He treaded slowly behind her, satisfied she collected the gifts. Reminding her to say, *thank you* would be asking for too much considering she was still mad at him—after a week. He had taken her for granted, and boy, she had made him sweat it out for seven days.

"Would you like something to eat and drink?"

"Are you sure?" At the moment, he was not certain where he stood with her, so eating and drinking might be a dumb idea.

Kiarra raised one eyebrow.

"Yes please." Of course, he changed his mind really quick. If saying yes was what she wanted to hear, it's what was best. All he wanted was to have her back.

"How did you get, Taleisha to turn on me?"

"Kia, it wasn't my intention to hurt you."

Closing her hands around the huge teddy bear, she pressed her face against the cuddly toy.

"Feels so soft. I love it."

Many tender jolts coursed through his body. Although if she had pressed her face against his chest, he would have been thrilled, he took comfort from the fact she loved his gift. That sufficed–for now.

He smiled. "I'm glad you do. I've missed you so much, Kia. I hate that I lied to you. I'm working in sales in my own company at the moment because I want to understand first hand what's going on in the market without the pile of paperwork shielding me, or reports and explanations that don't make sense."

Kiarra peeled out her head from the teddy bear side, set it down on the grey sofa and faced him. She then unwrapped her gift and gushed.

"Luxury chocolate feast! Lovely."

"It's a little token to say how sorry I am."

After she put down the chocolate box, she set her hands on her hips and pinned him with a direct gaze.

"Why didn't you tell me if that's your explanation?"

"Because I didn't want word to get out, I was working undercover in my own company."

"Oh, so you were afraid I'd sell you out to the press, or what?"

Clasping his hand in front of him, a humbling pose he hoped, he cleared his throat. "No, not you."

"Then why didn't you tell me? You didn't trust me?"

Raising his right hand, he shook his head.

"I trusted you. I just wanted to get away from the spotlight, from being the CEO. I liked what we had."

Shaking her head with vigour, she removed the towel and her dark curls bounced around her ears. He wanted to drive his fingers inside her tresses.

"You deceived me. That's what we had. You made me feel like an idiot! All I'd to do was look you up on the internet. But I didn't. I was too busy trying to save you from yourself."

"I'm glad you didn't." He covered the paces between them. "I hate to see the hurt in your eyes, Kia. I didn't mean to upset you. I was selfish."

"Yes, you were. And I'm very mad at you. That sweet-eyed giant teddy bear will not save you from my wrath, Ryder. Not even the chocolate can."

"Honestly, I get why you're mad at me. I'm just asking for a second chance."

"No. You didn't trust me to confide in me even after I dated you for months. Not three days. Before that, I was in and out of your condo for months. This whole thing is one-sided and I'm done."

His heart split in half. Clenching his teeth, he tried not to listen to the words climbing out of her lips. Because her eyes spewed disappointment, not hatred.

"What can I do to fix this mess?"

"Work it out yourself," she said with a shrug.

"I'm not done with you, Kiarra Wright."

Moving her head forward and backward, she lifted both eyebrows. "Excuse me?"

His stubborn girlfriend pushed her head forward as her eyes ignited with the passionate spark he had not seen in a week.

"You heard right. Kiarra, you strolled into my life when I was broken and had no one there for me. You picked me up and didn't take no for an answer over and over again. You pushed through until you touched my heart, shook out the icicles, filled it with passion and owned it. Now, you don't get to walk away when my fire is burning just for you."

Eyes wide with surprise, Kiarra dropped her hands and moved toward him. Standing in front of him now, she poked his chest with one finger.

"So, there's a fire burning in your lying, cold-hearted chest for me, Ryder Blade?"

He grabbed her waist, lifted her and hugged her tight, growling, "I'll show you."

While she giggled, he coated her robust lips with his mouth and kissed her for long minutes until they both needed air. She smelled of fresh flowers and wine.

"His name is Ryder by the way."

"Whose name?" Kiarra moaned, pecking at his bottom lip as she cupped his face with both hands.

"The bear."

"Definitely not. She's a girl and her name's Kiarra!"

"That can't be correct, considering I picked him out. I would know the gender of the bear."

"The bear has no erection!" she disputed.

They laughed so much their stomachs hurt.

Tightening his arms around her hips, he breathed in the rosy fragrance along her neck.

"It feels so right to have you back in my arms, Kia."

Twirling her fingers behind his head, she leaned closer. "I missed you so much, I couldn't return to my condo."

His mom was right. "Was I haunting you?"

"More than that. Your buzzy laughter and piercing gaze tormented me, not to mention your macho cologne." She inhaled, giggling afterward.

Amused by her confession, he chuckled.

"Good. That's what I like to hear."

Lifting her in his arms higher, he cuddled her face with his lips, whispering.

"I'm not letting you go again, babe."

"Sounds like what I want to hear, Ryder Blade. Although, you'll get sentenced in a moment."

He mocked gasped. "Your honour, please be lenient with me as I'm a first-time offender."

Kiarra laughed so much, her head fell backward with abandon. With her laughter so infectious, he joined her.

"I've taken your lenient plea into consideration, Mr. Blade," Kiarra said after she quit laughing. "You're hereby sentenced to one year of probation and a hundred hours of community service."

"Wow! At your service your honour. Will I be serving in your chambers?"

"You wish, Ryder. But you'll brew *Rich Earth Coffee* and get me pancakes, or muffins, or doughnut every morning at seven, so I can be on my A-game at work."

"Happy to serve you freshly-brewed *Rich Earth Coffee* every morning along with pancakes. Will that be the end of my community service, your honour?"

"Yes, until I think of something else you can do–"

He dropped his hands to the top of her butt cheeks, sliding down in slow bites. "I could do more." He placed his lips on top of her cleavage.

"I see you've been watching *All Rise*, hmm?"

"Had to after you abandoned me, your honour. The female star judge, *Simone Missick* had a stinging resemblance to you, I couldn't wait to kiss your lips."

"Because she's black and a fellow Detroiter?"

"Yeah. Also, you're curvy, very beautiful, feisty and warm-hearted. I wonder why I never watched *All Rise* before I met you."

Kiarra bent her head and trapped his lips with her tongue. He let her take the lead and she silenced him with a lasting kiss that saw him shudder from his head to his groin. His heart swung around in his chest. Powerful strokes of desire lashed through him.

"That's for saying such amazing things about me."

"My mom sends her regards." He carried her to lie down on his chest on the three-cushion leather sofa.

Kiarra's eyes popped as she tried to sit up.

"Are you joking, Ryder?"

Chuckling, he nodded, keeping her entire body flattened on his own with both hands. "Yeah." Though all he had to do to satisfy his arousal was to untie her robe, he did not. There would be time for that. Now he was content and elated to keep her in his arms.

"You and your mom worked things out in the end?"

"Yeah."

She smacked his chest. "Not, *yeah*. Fill me in."

He gave her details about his mom's visit ending with, "For the first time in decades, Lindsay Blade showed up when I needed her most." He left out the part where he sobbed like a baby.

"When it mattered," she added, hugging his neck tight as she showered his cheeks with many juicy kisses. "Oh, how you've matured, Ryder Blade. That's wonderful!"

"Thank you. I got a boot to my ass when you stormed out. I fell in line because I finally understood how miserable my mom felt for years due to the fact I didn't listen to her explanations, or forgive her. Every day you kept me in the dark, it was a reminder of what I'd done to my mom. It hurt again and again."

"So, I'm responsible for reconciling mom and son?"

"Yes. You made me see things clearly."

"No, I can't take the glory," she denied quickly. "God did the reconciliation.

"You think so? You think God's interested in me?"

"I'm happy for you, Ryder. Your mom deserves a break and so do you. I know God is interested in you because he loves you, Ryder. God is love."

He pinched her nose and released it. "Well, Lindsay has requested we have dinner with her next Saturday evening at her hotel. Are you up for it?"

"Do I have a choice?" This time she succeeded in sitting upright on his thigh.

"Yes and no." He chocked his upper body on his elbows, pleased to simply be with her.

She smiled. "Meaning what?"

"Meaning she'll not take no for an answer."

"Wait, is this an official, meet-my-mom kind of dinner date?"

He laughed at the uneasy expression on her face. Leaning forward, he smoothened the creases across her brow with his lips. "Hey, what's the matter, Kia?"

She worried her bottom lip. "I'm nervous."

He caressed her lips with his fingers before pasting his mouth over hers. As he nibbled the corner of her lips, he crooned. "There's no need to be nervous. You've met her. Lindsay Blade likes you already."

"Are you sure?" She made sexy soft sounds.

"Yes, I'm sure. You made a good impression the first time."

He sucked her top lip as his hard length pounded between his legs.

"Did your mom say she liked me?"

"Not in the exact words but she helped me win you back. So that's a definite yes, she likes you, a lot."

"What? How did that happen?"

"Long story. But believe me, she did. Dinner with my mom on Saturday? Yes?"

She nodded. "Yes. I'll be honoured. But you've got to do something for me first."

"Anything?"

"Come with me to church tomorrow. Please. You need faith to get on with me and, my family long term, trust me."

Grinning, he nodded. "Abandoning me isn't in your future plans for me, right?" Suddenly the thought of meeting her family did not sound petrifying.

"No. I'm just saying, religion is a big deal to me. This won't work if you don't try to have a relationship with God. When I'm upset with you like with anything else that bothers me in life, I run to God and I pray through his Son, Jesus Christ. I get peace and honestly, the big guy answers."

"Fine. Let's do it. I'll go with you to church."

She squealed, hugging him tighter.

Taking a cue, from her passion, he lodged a kiss inside her mouth, the type that he dragged on for a while and involved a passionate party dance of naked moist tongues. And in the heat of the moment, he peeled back her robe and snagged her nipple with his mouth.

Chapter 14 – All Messed Up

Kiarra

𝒦𝒾𝒶𝓇𝓇𝒶 applied a smoky shimmering eyeshadow to her eyelids with the brush in her hand and added a different shade to the crease line. Tonight, her dark hair acted as a setting to tie her deep brown eyes and smoky eye makeup together. With an eyeliner, she drew a dark line across her bottom eyelid one after the other before topping it up with dark grey eyeshadow.

In contrast, she wore a bright red lipstick after she edged her lips with a deep red shade liner. She leaned forward to peer at herself in the dresser mirror. Satisfied with the progress so far, with the blackest mascara she bought specifically for tonight, she volumized and lengthened her eyelashes for a dramatic look. For tonight's appearance, she ditched her false lashes.

There was one thing on Kiarra's mind. It was to keep Ryder's eyes on her throughout the date, his mom's presence notwithstanding.

Just then, the doorbell went off in rapid sequence.

Letting out air from her lips, she made her way to the door, her purse in hand. One more time, she pressed one palm along her cleavage and slid down to her belly. Swallowing her nerves, she opened the door.

Ryder froze. Moments after, he licked his lips. With wide eyes he wandered from her face to her cleavage, made a stop at her belly and hips before ending at her feet. Just as slowly, his eyes came up again to her face.

She cocked her head. Was her makeup too much? Did he approve of her shimmering dress? A pleated-cape-sleeve bodycon in mid-pink. It was elegant and she felt great. Securing her belly and curves with a body shaper ensured she fit in the dress like a glove. Her pulse ticked like she had run a marathon. Air got lost somewhere in her throat, so she swallowed.

"Damn!" he breathed out, hand on chest. "You look phenomenal!" His gaze, hot and appreciative lingered.

Meanwhile, she could not keep her eyes from admiring his remarkable features and appearance. Classic black shirt, tailored dark pants topped with a stylish blue blazer. No tie. His hair was set in place and his shoes were a black choice, overall, his appearance was very tempting.

Smiling, she gushed. "You look fabulous in your smart casual dinner outfit. I'm speechless and you smell like I should sleep with you."

Ryder stepped forward. He chuckled and wrapped his arms around her in the most intimate hug. "Let's skip dinner and get on to it. I've got a hard-on."

Her heart thundered and she trembled. Aroused, she shook her head. "And keep your mom wating?"

"Not a good idea. After dinner?" He winked. "This hairstyle suits your perfect face."

"Thank you." She had settled for a side braided ponytail after trying on four other hairstyles.

"I'm going to wrestle with my lips till after dinner."

Pouting her lips, she leaned back with her arms wrapped behind his waist. "I don't follow."

"Your lips are appealing but I can't kiss you yet."

"After dinner kiss it is. Let's go impress your mom."

"But I'm tearing your lips down after that."

He cuddled her shoulders, gulping in her fragrance.

"Yeah." Giggling, she fell into step beside him. Then she had a memory recall. "One moment."

She hurried back inside to collect the bouquet of flowers and a bottle of red wine, her gifts for his mom.

"Wow!" He pecked her cheeks. "You're thoughtful."

The moment they arrived at *The US Grant, a Luxury Collection Hotel* along Broadway a while later, Kiarra panicked. She tightened her fingers around her boyfriend's. He pulled her into a tight embrace and kissed her side face and cheeks until she was calm.

"My mom likes you, Kia. And even if she doesn't, you're my girl. Have fun tonight."

Nodding, she smiled. "It would mean a lot to me if she accepted me as your girlfriend."

"She will. Stop fretting, my beautiful Kia."

"Okay." His words calmed her nerves somewhat. Yet no matter what he said if his mom disapproved, she doubted she and Ryder would have a future together. Family feuds were not her forte. Her family was her life.

Taking her hand in one of his, Ryder winked, kissed the corner of her lips before leading her to the *Grant Grill Restaurant* inside the 5-star hotel in *Gaslamp Quarter* in Downtown San Diego.

Gooey sensations turned up the hairs along her spine as they walked toward Ryder's mom, seated at a table near the handcrafted wooden wall décor. Lindsay, garbed in a black dress was not on her own. Another young couple was already chatting with her.

"Did I miss something?" Kiarra queried. "I thought we were having dinner with your mom, only?"

Ryder narrowed his gaze at first. When recognition dawned, he laughed, whispering. "That's Alana and Alex, her other half. She's a doll. Don't worry."

Nervous, Kiarra took in a wild breath, blinked and swallowed. One member of the family had now turned into three. Was she ready to face his entire family? *Whether, or not I'm ready, the time is now.*

Once they reached the table, Ryder reintroduced Kiarra to his mom, which was a good thing.

"Good evening, Mrs. Blade. Nice to meet you again. These are for you." Kiarra handed the gifts to Lindsay, who gawked at the flowers and wine bottle as if she had never received gifts in her entire life.

"Thank you." The older woman's eyes welled up, before she set down the gifts and swept Kiarra into a welcoming hug. "You look gorgeous!"

"Hi, you must be Kiarra," the younger, auburn-haired woman with pale green eyes, said beaming as she opened her arms wide. "Come here."

Gasping with both relief and surprise, Kiarra loosened her arms from Lindsay's and rushed toward Alana. Out of the corner of her eyes, she saw Lindsay also hug her son. The unease in Kiarra's stomach from moments ago vanished.

"Hi Alana," Kiarra greeted, smiling afterward. "Nice to meet you. Ryder says lovely things about you."

Attired in an aqua pleated gown, Alana's eyes bulged as she chuckled. "He does?" When she spoke that way, she sounded very much like Ryder.

"Meet my husband, Alexander Watson. Everyone calls him Alex," Alana said, beaming.

Wearing a white shirt over dark pants, the tall white guy, grinned. Standing a few steps from the spotlight,

Kiarra's face reflected off Alex's bald head as he extended his head.

"Hi Kiarra. Call me, Alex. Like Alana said, everyone does. Great to meet you," Alex hailed.

A smiling Kiarra shook his hand. "Hello Alex. The pleasure is mine."

"Come and give me another hug, Kiarra," Ryder's mom said with a short laugh. "If it weren't for you, I might still have been in the dog house."

Very relieved this was not the strained, formal dinner she had anticipated, Kiarra hugged Lindsay.

"How are you doing?" the older woman asked.

Full of gratitude to Lindsay for her warm welcome, Kiarra pecked the amiable older woman's cheeks. "I'm doing great. How are you holding up?"

"Aww, you're such a kind soul," said Lindsay, leaning back. "I'm blessed. Come, sit here beside me."

Standing on the other side, a laughing Ryder hugged his sister and dropped a peck on her hair, a medium brown shade that gave off plenty of warmth.

Kiarra loved the sight of brother and sister expressing their love for each other. Moving on from that, Ryder did a masculine handshake and a wide grin exchange with Alex. The atmosphere was great. The vibe was upbeat in the stunning Art Deco setting.

Around the long table for six, Lindsay Blade guided Kiarra to sit on her left side, while Alana and Alex were positioned on Lindsay's right. If Ryder had sat on Lindsay's right, they would have been separated by his mom. That would not have been ideal anyway.

Ryder, not bothered by the seating plan pulled out Kiarra's seat first. When she was comfortable, he sat on the beige fabric covered chair next to hers.

"Ryder, it's lovely to see you take care of Kiarra," Alana noted with a smile of approval.

Kiarra curved her neck to stare at her boyfriend.

"Isn't he always the gentleman?" Kiarra teased to poke the bear.

His sister made a my-mouth-is-zipped hand gesture before she said. "Always the gentleman, yes."

Ryder grinned, his broad shoulders settled nicely in his fitted jacket gave him a superior air of importance.

A waitress appeared. "Hello, I'm Shea, I'll be taking care of you all today. What would you like to drink?"

"Hi Shea," Lindsay took the lead. "A blue martini for me. Ask my family what they each want and we'll go from there."

Minutes later, with all the drinks order taken, Shea left them to chatter.

"What a surprise to see you two in San Diego." Ryder pushed his gaze to his sister and her husband.

"I know," Alex responded. "I tagged along because I was told I'd get to meet your girlfriend."

Everyone responded with loud chuckles.

"I invited them to join us because I wanted this to be a long overdue family reunion," Lindsay explained. "After I met Kiarra at your place, I was so impressed with the way she handled the conflict situation between us, I told your sister all about it."

"And I was dying to meet you," Alana confirmed with a curious twinkle in her eyes. "Especially after I heard my brother cried because of you."

Kiarra gasped, zeroing in on Ryder. "You cried?"

Grinning, Ryder shook his head. "That's a secret. My mom can't keep a secret. Now I know."

They all split their sides laughing.

Drinks were delivered and the food order was taken. When the waitress was done and they had raised their glasses to cheer, Kiarra returned to the discussion on the table.

"Wait, when was this? I didn't know you cried for me. I should've made a recording."

"Yeah. It means you're pretty special to Ryder," Alana confirmed with a firm shake of her head.

"And you're very special to us, as a family," his mom added. "And I wanted to say thank you for putting up with my son. Trust me, I know how sweet he is on a bad day."

Of course, they all laughed.

"I didn't realize my mom was making me the subject at the family dinner date," Ryder whispered in her ear. "My temper is perfect. Is it not babe?"

While shivers sped through her spine at his warm breath, the others hid knowing smiles. Everyone had heard her boyfriend's deep-throated whisper.

"Time to tell all. Where did you stumble on Kiarra?" Alex directed his gaze across the table to Ryder.

Instead of answering, her boyfriend threw her a naughty wink. "Please do the honours, Kia."

"All eyes turned to her."

"Tell us the story of your first meeting," Lindsay encouraged with a refreshing smile. "We're prying."

The scene that set them on a collision course came rushing back to her. She took in a deep breath and recounted their awkward first meeting.

"Don't laugh. We met at a barbecue meeting at the condo building where we both live. As an ice breaker, I asked Ryder if he wanted to marry me."

Not one, or two, everyone seated at the table choked on their drinks with the exception of herself.

Even Ryder coughed out his drink. Laughing now, Kiarra glanced sideways at her boyfriend. "Why are you choking? You knew what was coming?"

"I didn't realize you were going to lead with that one," came his comical feedback laced with a wink.

"Did that really happen, Kiarra?" Alex and Alana chorused their faces animated.

"Did it?" Lindsay questioned her hazel eyes bright with disbelief. "Did you ask Ryder to marry you?"

"How do you think I took it?" Ryder chirped.

"What was going through your mind at the time?" Alana queried eager to hear the spicy details.

Kiarra shrugged. "Nothing in particular. I wanted Ryder to lighten his dark, mysterious mood."

"And what did you say, Ryder?" Alex queried.

"Not in a million years," her boyfriend croaked.

Alana spilled her drink from her mouth, her husband had to plug the drips with a cotton napkin.

Lindsay nodded. "Very interesting. So, how did you go from that, to crying and, to your happy place now?"

Ryder stared into Kiarra's eyes for a long moment. "I realized I was a fool." He steadied his gaze on hers, temporarily excluding others from their silent conversation. "She had the patience of a saint, a generous heart of gold and she was drop-dead gorgeous anyway, so I fell hard and long for her."

"Whoa!" came the loud whispers around the table.

Emotions scattered their sweet fangs around Kiarra's cleavage. Discarding the restraint on her thoughts, she leaned forward. Ryder, read her intentions and, met her past the half-way mark as he plugged her wobbly lips with his own steady, soft one.

A subtle clap sounded around the table.

"Aww. You two are so good together," Alana praised, sloping her head on her husband's shoulder.

"Love is such a beautiful thing to see," Lindsay added. "But you must protect it at all costs. Never put anything ahead of your love for each other. I did and I regret it. I want to see your relationship blossom into marriage. Have you thought about getting married?"

Their reply was aborted because their first course arrived. Afterward, the main course followed without a gap. While they waited for the last course, Lindsay recollected and repeated her question.

Kiarra had no clue what to say. Yes, she wanted to get married, but Ryder had not said anything more since their date on his yacht many weeks ago, when she told him about her wish to have a family.

"Mom, we'll let you know when the time comes." Ryder took the lead. "You'll get an invitation."

Ignoring his son's remark, Lindsay took hold of Kiarra's hand on the table.

"Are you ready to get married? Do you want to have a family?" Lindsay's expression was earnest.

Kiarra did not have to look at Ryder for a cue on this one. This was her dream. "Yes. Ryder knows my thoughts on that. I want to get married when the time is right and I want my own family. It's my dream."

Lindsay tapped her wrist. "Thank you. That means a lot. Not every woman can handle my son. But you can. That gives me peace of mind."

"I agree," Alana added her two cents opinion.

Alex nodded. "I concur."

It was incredible to have Ryder's family ready to accept her as part of their family.

"Honestly, you've got an amazing son, Mrs. Blade." Words she had not meant to say almost nudged out of

Kiarra's lips as an overwhelming wave of tender emotions raided her heart. She swallowed them before adding. "Ryder means a lot to me."

Her boyfriend tucked his hand under her curls and stroked her neck. A warm wind rushed to her butt.

"Do you think your parents will accept, Ryder with open arms?" It was Lindsay asking with a frown on her ivory smooth brow.

"Yes. If I love Ryder, they'll love him," Kiarra stated.

"Do you love him?" Alex's gaze pinned on Kiarra's.

Kiarra had lured herself into a tight spot with that one. Clearing her throat, she blinked a few times.

"Can I skip that question?" Kiarra begged.

"Okay. Give her a break, Alex," Alana said, coming to her rescue. "Tell us about your siblings, Kiarra."

"I've got two siblings, an older sister, Jalicia who's married and lives in New Jersey and my older brother, Deiondre who's single and lives in Atlanta."

"That's good." Nodding, Lindsay linked her fingers.

"What have you been up to?" Ryder asked his sister.

"I've got a lot going on at the moment. But I'm coping." Alana grinned. "Busy, busy."

"Planning to start a family soon, I hope?" Lindsay dropped the hint buttering it up with a pleasant smile.

Alex and Alana exchanged secret glances that everyone noticed.

"Spill. What's going on?" Ryder pushed with a sneaky grin. "Don't deny it. I saw that look."

Laughing, Alex nodded. "We're expecting a baby."

"Thank the good Lord," Lindsay said beaming before everyone hugged and congratulated the couple.

"Are you religious now, Mom?" Ryder queried.

"Without a marriage and with my kids out of the nest, what do you think I do in my ample spare time?"

"Don't know. Drink tea at the club, or something."

"The Lord has been good to me these past couple of years. I was pressed on every side by troubles, but I wasn't crushed. I was perplexed, but not driven to despair because Jesus Christ found me and picked me up. How do you think I got brave to find you and asked for your forgiveness? You should try talking to him sometime, Ryder."

Kiarra squeezed her boyfriend's arms. "Oh, don't worry, Mrs. Blade. Ryder attends church with me."

"Really?" Alex and Alana spoke in unison.

"Do you love going to church now, Ryder?" His mom wanted to know.

"I'm still finding my way to God," Ryder clarified. "I wish you'd taken me to church when I was young."

Feeling the need to intervene, Kiarra side kicked Ryder's feet to keep him quiet. It worked. He stopped talking. The last thing anyone at the table needed tonight was to play referee between mom and son.

"How did you and Alex meet?" Kiarra trailed her eyes to Alana.

Slanting her head to her husband, Ryder's sister giggled. "We met at a restaurant. We were both seated at different tables, but we couldn't take our eyes off each other."

They all had a good laugh about Alex and Alana's sweet love story. From then on, it was fun getting to know each other until it was time to say goodbye. Before that, Ryder paid the bill and handed out a hefty tip to the attending waiter. Like fine wine, her boyfriend grew more mature every day.

While everyone exchanged hugs and promised to stay in touch, Kiarra replayed every moment of the evening in her head. From their warm welcome to the spectacular Four-Diamond cuisine to the excellent company and merrymaking. A good feeling nested in the pit of her stomach. It was a sign her relationship was on good ground.

From behind, Ryder enfolded her with both arms, twisting her around quickly. Her head spun with giddy excitement. Giggling at the sudden movement, she flung her arms around his neck.

Ryder lunged at her mouth as he promised, tearing down her walls as he sweetened her lips with the taste from his tongue and the deeper emotions in his heart.

Chapter 15 – Don't Do It

Kiarra

After curling up in her boyfriend's arms on the white centrepiece rug in her living room, Kiarra now nestled her head on his chest. Lying at an angle to her, Ryder had one arm resting above his shoulder to cup his head from behind. Ryder was hot. Morning. Noon, or Evening. In fact, his night time appeal was extraordinary. Skewing her head, she caressed the inside of his bicep.

His eyes brushed hers with a tenderness she had come to treasure. She looked forward to spending most weekends with him because it was pure bliss.

"You're stunning, Kia even after a day out spent in the sun."

They had spent the entire first Saturday in November on *Solana Beach*, along the northern coast of San Diego and only got back an hour ago.

"Aww. Thank you, honey." She slipped her fingers to his armpit and tweaked the dark brown hair. The patch was not bushy but it was softer than his beard. The hairy skin dispatched shivers to her breasts.

"I love that, Kia. But your fingers are ticklish."

"Are you ticklish?" she mocked with a wide grin.

Puckering her lips, she swept her fingertips along his armpit mimicking feather light caresses. He rolled away from her, laughing as he did. She crawled on the faux fur sheepskin rug, following him behind, tickling him until he trapped her hands.

Ryder pulled her to lie beneath him. He laid flush against her and ground his mouth over hers, pinning down her hands. Though caught beneath his toned body, she leaned her head forward to deepen the kiss. Over and over, their lips clashed and met again singing a love song without words. He crushed his chest on top of her boobs, pressing down hard and bringing a ton of tremors along with it.

With her pulse whirling, her heart thundered. Between her thighs, she felt his bulge harden and thump. Longing for more, she clenched her muscles as she felt wetness spring on to her underwear.

Moaning as her yearning for him deepened, she set her hands free and pushed her fingers under his black T-shirt. Across his back, she palmed his muscles.

But Ryder put a stop to it. He rolled off her, sat up and avoided her gaze. "I'm crazy about you, Kia."

"And you know you drive me insane with need."

"What am I going to do with you, babe?"

Ryder turned his head sideways and tilted toward his left shoulder.

"Is something wrong?" She could not read the sudden sadness in his tone.

Now what? After their dinner date with his family, the past three months had gone by without a hitch in their relationship.

"There's something I've got to tell you, Kia. It's been weighing on my mind."

His tone was neither playful nor flirty. In fact, he sounded ominous. Her nerves tightened with fear. Whatever he had to say scared her already.

"Ryder? Are you breaking up with me?"

He rolled his shoulders, a sure sign of anxiety. "No! Of course not. But promise me you won't be mad."

For a few seconds he buried his face in his hands.

"What are you ashamed to share with me?" She paused, wondering what had her boyfriend's neck flushed a bright red. "I can't make you a firm promise. Did you cheat on me?"

"No! I'll never cheat on you."

"OK. I'll listen without judging."

"I went to prison." His lips wobbled somewhat as he blurted out the shocking news.

Kiarra felt a rock hit her head. Dazed, not in a good way, she sat on her butt. Of all the things she expected, that was not on the list—at all.

"W-what? For what?" she stuttered.

Ryder tapped his feet. "It was an accident. We were seventeen."

Narrowing her eyes, she queried. "*We*? How many of you?"

"Jerrad and I. We'd had a little too much to drink. He was driving my car at the time."

If Ryder went to prison for an accident it must have been a bad one. "Did you hit someone?"

With his head bowed, Ryder groaned as if he was in pain. "Yes. A pro footballer. I ruined his career. He had only been a pro for a year."

"But you weren't the one at the wheels. Wait, so, you went to prison for drunk driving?"

"For possession of class C drugs; anabolic steroids and speed because they were found in my car."

"Were you on drugs too?"

"No, I wasn't. But Jerrad was. He wanted to build his muscles."

"You didn't have to go to prison. Why didn't you tell the police the drugs belonged to Jerrad?"

"Because friends don't do that, Kia. I've known Jerrad since preschool. He's my brother in every sense. I couldn't do that to him. He had been booked for reckless driving and driving under the influence of alcohol and other drugs. I couldn't hang him out to dry."

Kiarra stared wide-eyed as her head processed the horrible newsflash.

"In other words, you went to jail because of your loyalty to your friend?"

"I went to jail because I shouldn't have allowed him to drive. I knew we'd alcohol in our system. I knew he had drugs in the car. It was my car and therefore my responsibility. I should've known better. But I was young, reckless and feeling abandoned. Drinking and partying was fun until it wasn't. Jail was a nightmare."

"This is all messed up, Ryder. Hold on. You were seventeen, why weren't you sent to Juvie?"

"We ended up in Juvenile Court for months at first. In Colorado, you can be tried as adults from sixteen. After Juvie, we got tried as adults, ended up in prison for a year. I was an idiot. I made a mistake and I did my time. What I couldn't live with was the fact I ruined a man's career because of my recklessness."

Kiarra got on her feet and paced.

"This is a little too much. Why are you just saying this to me now? We're meeting my family in three weeks for Thanksgiving dinner. What am I supposed to do? Call it off?"

"I wanted you to know everything about me. It's the guilt I carried around until you came into my life."

"What? The guilt fell off your shoulders when I walked through the door?" she snapped. "You've had eight months to tell me. Why keep it from me?"

Her heart was hammering out of her chest. Just when she thought they had gone past every difficulty in their relationship, he dug out a new one.

"Sort of, yes. There was something refreshing, comforting about your presence. I didn't remember my guilt, or my past. I should have told you sooner."

"Why did you take responsibility for everything?"

"I wanted to atone for what we'd done."

"So, you earned a criminal record for something you didn't do, Ryder? This is seriously crazy!"

"Entering the car and driving that night changed the course of another man's life. Instead of a pro footballer, he now coaches. I've got to live with that. Sometimes, I think I don't deserve to have the life I've got, owning my business and being a success story."

"At least, he's alive and has a career. Ryder, you've worked hard and turned your life around. You've earned it. Give yourself some credit and stop wearing the guilty label."

"Does that mean you're not mad at me?"

"It means you've paid for your mistakes in full. Look ahead and stop looking behind."

"I want you in my future, Kia. Can you forgive me for not telling you earlier?"

"What I want to know is why you didn't? This is a big deal to me and will be to my family."

"It's something I'm ashamed of, something I don't want any woman to know about me except I'm serious with her. With a past like mine, people judge harshly as if going to prison was a treat and not a living hell."

Staring at her boyfriend's remorseful gaze, she wanted to say everything was fine. But in her heart, she knew it might not be great going forward.

"Well, I'm not *people*. You didn't give me a chance to make my own decision about it. I've got to think about all of this, Ryder. Now I've got to worry about telling my family. My brother and mom would probably have a fit. This is all too much."

Ryder took her right hand and pulled her into his arms. She did not expect that after his dark confessions. What she needed was space to think. But he caged her body with hands that made her feel unbelievable things she could not describe.

After she stood stiff in his arms for a few moments, savage heat from his biceps and chest diced her stiff walls and she relaxed and pressed against him. She folded her hands around his waist, pushed her fingers up to his upper back and caressed his tense muscles.

Confused at feeling strong emotions for him despite what he just told her, the following words dripped from her lips.

"Ryder Blade, you're a man of many parts. Why couldn't you be simple, without complications?"

He stroked her back and shoulders with fingers that knew just how to start a flame in her body. Her boobs, now pushed against his chest hardened with desire. And her nipples ached for his touch.

"Because this is who I am and I'm meant to spend the rest of my life with you, Kia."

She threw her head back to gape at his eyes.

"What did you just say?"

"This may not be the right time to say it, but I'm telling you right now that I'm falling in love with you,

Kiarra Wright. I love everything about you. I love the little and big things about you. Please don't leave me because of my past."

Triple level thrill coursed through her heart. "You're not been fair to me right now. Piling it on when you've just dropped one bomb and I'm trying to wrap my head around it. I need some time to think."

He inhaled sharply. "Don't do it, Kia. I know you're disappointed in me. You've got every right to be. Don't take too long because I can't go on without you. That's a fact and I'm not ashamed to say it."

"Okay. I hear you. I really do. Thank you for telling me about your past. I would've hated to find out from someone else."

Heaviness almost replaced desire inside her chest.

His eyes lingered on her lips.

As torn as she was, she hungered for his kisses.

Seconds ticked past while they stood with their hands tangled around each other and their eyes penetrated each other's heart.

Just when she thought he would not kiss her, Ryder slanted his head and hard-pressed his mouth to hers. He dispersed nearly enough flames to flush out the doubts and confusion in her head. Not wanting their intimacy to end, she sucked his top and bottom lips. He sharpened his caresses inside her mouth. Their noses did not get in the way as they kissed deeply as if it was their first time. Her heart roared with greed and grief because her boyfriend tasted like delicious wine that was going out of production.

He moulded her waist and hips with potent hands.

Sobbing softly, she roamed around his back, spreading her fingers along every rigid muscle he owned. Shockwaves boomed past her boobs and rushed to her stomach. She shuddered against him even after he ended the kiss.

His fingers trembled against her skin.

In that moment, she believed in her heart Ryder was in love with her. It was safer for her to lean on him because her legs were not strong enough to hold her quivering body. Lightning and, thunder bolts blazed through every part of her body each time he kissed her, or caught her in his arms. He made her feel things she only dreamed about and heard about.

How could she let Ryder go now?

Being an ex-convict was not something you shook off. It stuck to you like glue. Her family would raise a storm if they found out. And she knew the moral thing to do was to walk away from him. But her heart was adamant it was the wrong thing to do.

"I need a break, Ryder."

He nodded. "For how long?"

"Maybe two weeks."

"Two weeks?" Rubbing his hands over his head, he squatted at her feet. "Please Kia. I get that you need time to process all this. I understand that, trust me. Please don't run away from me."

What could she say?

Chapter 16 – Follow Your Heart

Kiarra

After agonizing about what to do with the bombshell prison-term news Ryder dropped on her laps almost two weeks ago, Kiarra finally decided to confide in her mom. Crying had not resolved anything in fourteen days. One thing she did not do was to chat to her friends about Ryder's criminal past. She had felt the need to protect his privacy.

Kiarra pressed her mom's number on her cell phone and waited for her to answer.

Mabel Wright responded with an excited, "Hello, baby! How are you doing over there in San Diego?"

Kiarra immediately burst into tears.

"Hey, baby, what's the matter?" Her mom sounded alarmed.

At the back of her mind, Kiarra wondered what triggered the flood of tears. Maybe it was her mom's loving voice and familiar perkiness.

"Pull yourself together, my baby and tell me what's going on."

Sniffing and cleaning her face with her pyjama top sleeve, Kiarra recounted her conversation with Ryder. She did not leave out any of the salacious details. To her surprise, her mom did not interrupt, not once, which was unusual.

When Kiarra was done, Mabel cleared her throat.

"Everyone's got a past, Kiarra. He was a teenager."

Kiarra's chest lightened with relief.

"You know how much trouble teens in Detroit get into by the time they're twelve. Has this man, Ryder turned from his mistake? Has he got a good life now?"

"Yes, Mama. Ryder's the CEO of *Rich Earth Coffee*. He built the company from scratch. He's done good for himself. For our first date, he surprised me with a helicopter ride across San Diego. We flew all the way to LA for dinner. He's a romantic at heart, Mama."

"Good. That's a positive thing. If he has learnt from his mistakes and made a good life for himself, you can't punish him again after he's served his prison time. Does he still do drugs?"

"No, Mama. He never did drugs. It was his friend."

"That's a relief, Kiarra. An addict is another matter entirely. How do you feel when you're with him.?"

"I feel like a beautiful queen when I'm with Ryder. No one, and nothing else matters. We share a deep emotional bond. Ryder's so attentive, caring and most importantly he makes me laugh. He gets me and I love that about him."

"Do you make him happy?"

"I think so. He laughs a lot when we're together. And he begged me not to leave him. We were already set for him to meet you all at Thanksgiving."

"I know. We were looking forward to meeting him. Has Ryder told you he loves you?"

"Yes. But he said it at the same time he told me about his jail term. I was confused. I wasn't sure if he said that because he knew I was upset about his big bad criminal record."

"Listen to your heart, baby. You know him, I don't. In time, you'll find out if he truly loves you. Do you love, Ryder?"

A lengthy pause flowed back and forth.

"I don't know, Mama," she said at the end.

"Okay. If I'd asked you the same question three weeks ago what would you have said?"

"I would've said I was falling in love." That was a lie in itself because she had known the truth for a while.

"Let me rephrase that. Have you fallen out of love with him because of what he told you about his past?"

A heavy sigh rode out of Kiarra's mouth.

Kiarra and her mom were pretty close and she told her mom almost anything. But this was harder than she expected. Mabel Wright was great at asking difficult questions. The kind of questions that often helped her children figure out their jumbled thoughts.

"Mama, I really don't know. I'm more worried about what you, pops and everyone else will think about him. I miss Ryder so much. Every night, I cry to sleep. Though I've known him for less than a year, it feels like a lot longer."

"Forget about your family for a minute. Picture your life and, your future without him. Do you think you'll be happy without Ryder?"

Her heart broke and she started to cry again. Sniffing moments later, she shook her head.

"No, Mama. I can't picture my life without him."

"Then you know what to do. Follow your heart."

She exhaled slowly, smiling at the end of their chat. "You're not mad at Ryder for keeping me in the dark?"

"If you can let it go, we can, Kiarra. Make decisions so you don't have to live with regret."

Hmm "Thank you, Mama for making me feel a lot better. I miss you so much."

In all honesty, she had not expected her mom to take Ryder's imprisonment record on the chin.

"I'm glad you called. You know I'm always here for you, my baby. You've no idea how much I miss you."

"I know, Mama."

"Let's talk about Thanksgiving."

"What about it, Mama?"

"We can't all be together this year. You and Jalicia might have to celebrate it with your brother in Atlanta because he can't get away."

"We'll work it out. Don't worry about it. How are you doing? And how's pops?"

"I'm good, thank the good Lord who spares our lives each day. I've got no complaints. Your pop's giving me his usual trouble. Nothing I can't handle."

Kiarra chuckled. "What? Is he eating late and having a drink when you're not looking?"

Mabel snorted. "You know him well, your pops. Oh! He started driving me crazy mowing the lawn twice a week. It's the start of winter! The grass doesn't grow!"

Both women laughed.

"You've lived with him for so long, Mama. If you didn't kill him when we were young, I guess you can take a bit more, don't you think?"

"That's right. How often do you speak to your brother and sister anyway?" Always the same query.

"Not as often as you'd like. But we chat by texts almost every day."

"Text? What happened to phone calls?"

"And that too. Mama, someone's knocking. I've got to go. I love you a lot. Hug pops for me."

"If it's Ryder, him I know all about his past dirty dealings."

Kiarra beamed. "Mama, are you going to tell pops?"

"You want me to give him an abridged version?"

"Yes, Mama. What about Deiondre and Jalicia?"

"You handle your siblings. I'll handle your pops."

"Okay. Love you, Mama. Bye."

"God bless you, my baby."

"Bless you more, Mama."

"Amen," two of them said in unison.

Chapter 17 – Come Here

Ryder

Checking her reflection in the mirror above the fireplace, Kiarra cringed at the puffiness around her eyes. Crying daily in her heart and with tears mashing her eyes since her two-week separation from Ryder, she could not be an aspirant for the catwalk runway.

Her doorbell pealed again.

Shelving her mom's phone call that just ended, Kiarra dashed to her bathroom, opened the faucet and with both hands, splashed cold water on her face to reduce the puffiness. *Just Perfect!* It was refreshing. Her face cooled down instantly.

Meanwhile, the door bell ringing persisted.

Though she was not in the mood to meet anyone, she changed into her racer-back cotton sleepshirt. The light weight fabric wisped above her knees. As she hurried toward the front door, she shrugged on her satin night robe and belted it. Maybe she was gradually turning into Ryder Blade. A quick grin partied on her lips at the thought.

When she opened the door, Ryder stood there with a dark expression on his face.

"Your two weeks is up. Here I am again begging you, Kia. Please."

Happiness in every colour erupted throughout her body, so she started smiling.

Ryder's eyes widened. "Are we good, babe?"

Unable to hold back the glee wracking her body she burst out laughing. "My mom said, and I quote, *tell Ryder I know all about his past dirty dealings.*"

A sexy grin bloomed across his granite features. Then he frowned. "Wait. You told your mom about me? About everything?"

She nodded, laughing.

He ran one shaky hand through his hair. "Was she mad at me? Can I come in?"

Standing aside, she leaned against the door. Her boyfriend strode in, his steps unsure as his gaze darted to her face.

"Why? You scared of Mabel Wright?"

"Shouldn't I be? I never met her, now she knows all about my past."

"You want a drink?"

He blocked her way after she locked the door.

"What else did your mom say, Kia?"

Tired of watching him suffer, she grinned. "She said I should follow my heart."

Roaring with joy, he cupped his mouth with both hands. His hazel eyes glinted. "Are we good?"

"Yeah."

Ryder gathered her in his arms. Full of glee herself, she twisted her arms around his hips.

"Aww, someone is happy," she teased, pressing her side face to his pounding chest.

He tightened his hands around her back and growled above her head. In between his loud grunts, he kissed her hair and forehead.

"Lord, I missed your interfering ass in my life!"

She giggled hard, smacking his butt with one hand. "Nothing felt right in the last two weeks for me."

Without Ryder and his shenanigans, her life had been bland. She needed him. With Ryder, she was passionate and desire in its raw state knew her name She was a woman with a heart and soul designed to love him. For a long time, she had not felt this fiery heat for any guy. She had thought she could never feel this way again. Ryder had given her a great gift.

"I missed your scent, Kia. I missed you nagging me to clean up my kitchen. I missed you stretching out on the couch with me. I missed stroking your cellulite blessed thighs and thick legs. I missed kissing your lips, your body. I even missed you kissing your teeth."

Words she had not said in a very long time almost slipped out of her lips. She swallowed to lock them in. Her heart bumped inside her chest. The sound competed with Ryder's loud heartbeats.

"I'm sorry for our separation. I should've told you."

She patted his lips with one finger. "I love you, Ryder. I love you today. I know I'll love you tomor–"

Ryder swept her up in a wave of glory. While she laughed at his display of affection, he bowed his head and collected her mouth in a longing kiss that left her trembling for more. She traded passion for passion, blaze for blaze. Smoke from her scorching desire filled her nostrils and expanded in her chest.

"I'm crazy about you, Kiarra Wright. This is the best gift you've given me. Thank you, baby."

She threaded her arms around his neck and kept her lips pasted to his own.

"No. You've given me the best gift ever. I didn't think I could open up my heart to love anyone again.

In the last two weeks, I got clarity. I don't want to live without you."

"Please marry me, Kia."

A sharp gasp exploded from her lips while she clutched her chest with one hand. This was not happening. *Ryder's proposing to me?*

"What?" Maybe she did not hear the words right.

"Wait. I've got to do this right, babe." He tilted his arms, so she slid down. But he held on to her left hand while digging his other hand into his denim pocket.

"Did you plan this, Ryder?"

"Don't say anything, Kia. I've recited this proposal for a week."

Her fingers shading her lips quivered with love and anticipation. Nothing in his demeanour while he stood at the door pointed to the fact he intended to propose tonight. Her heart raced. She wished her mom was on the other end of the phone to listen to this moment in her life.

Ryder got out the cute blue box. He opened it. As he did, his eyes studied hers before he opened his lips.

"Before you marched into my world and into my life, I was not much company."

She giggled, rolling her eyes up and down. "That's putting it mildly."

"Yes. I thought I wasn't ready for a serious relationship. I thought I was done with love."

He echoed her inner fears. Words she had not told anyone because she did not want them to be true.

"It was the same for me, Ryder."

"What I'm saying is, I know I don't deserve you, Kia. I know I've not always made the best decisions. I'm not perfect and I make you mad. But I want to be a better version of myself for you."

Despite her self-talk not to cry, tears burned at the back of her eyes. Unshed, hot tears. She had not expected a humble Ryder to go on one bended knee.

"Before you end your speech, Ryder, can I ask you something first?"

He tilted his head back, parting his lips.

Ignoring the sexy slant of his posture, she shook her head. "Ryder Blade, will you marry me despite my shortcomings? I'm not promising you I'll be a perfect wife, but I'll try to be patient and love you forever."

One bold tear rolled down his cheek.

"Yes. I'll marry you if you'll have me, Kiarra wright. I promise I'll figure out how to love you the way you deserve for as long as forever. Will you marry me?"

Nodding, she laughed, cupping her mouth with one hand. "I will marry you, Ryder Blade today, tomorrow and the day after until we reach forever."

Chuckling, he pushed the glistening engagement ring on the fourth finger of her left hand. "Yes, I'll marry you, Kiarra Wright and forever, I'll be yours."

With her eyes filled with tears, fat drops splashed on his fingers. "It's so beautiful. My ring is gorgeous. I love it. Come here."

Overwhelmed with shock but eager to celebrate her surprise engagement, she tugged his arm. And her fiancé started to laugh as he folded her with his arms.

"Where in the world do you want to go?" He brushed his lips along her neck and slid his tongue under her chin. Desire blazed across her cleavage. Driven by need, she pushed her fingers under his T-shirt and palmed and stroked his sweet, hard skin.

"Mm...Somewhere exotic and beautiful!"

"Does this place have a name?"

"Mm-hmm. I saw it online. It's a woman's name."

He mimed her words along her earlobe sending love butterflies everywhere, teasing her senses.

"Like Kiarra's Island?" he crooned. "I'm assuming it's an Island. Sun. Sea. Ocean?"

"Um...Close. It's somewhere called, Stella Island."

Ryder arched his back, grinning. "Never heard of it. Are you sure it exists?"

"Sure. I like other islands. Bora Bora, Maldives."

"Great. Are we still going to meet your family?"

"Yes, but there's been a slight change."

"Bad change?"

She squeezed his lean waist. "No. My mom just told me Deiondre can't be in Detroit for Thanksgiving."

"Are we going to meet him separately then?"

"Yeah. Let me speak with Jalicia. She'll probably arrange for a separate dinner date for us at Deiondre's in Atlanta. Trust me, everyone's curious about you."

"Babe, I want to marry you as soon as I can."

"I love the sound of that. The feeling is mutual."

Ryder moulded her breasts with hands shaped to release high dose of pleasure through her body.

Moaning as quakes knocked the wind out of her ribs, her needy fingers crept up his chest. She pinned his nipples between her fingers. The soft peaks beaded in her hands. Heat surged down to the pit of her belly, pushing downward until she trembled.

"Things will work itself out," she groaned.

With hands long and lean, Ryder peeled back her robe from her shoulders. His warm breath coated her skin, clawing at her control. He followed his hand movements with his lips, pelting her skin with moist heat. She swiped her tongue around the inside of his bottom lip, rushing inside his mouth desperate to find the source of his rich sweetness and flavour.

When her robe slipped to the floor, it pooled around her feet. She arched her back into his arms and peered at his darkened eyes.

"I want you, Ryder, but–"

He dunked his head and captured the side of her mouth with his hot lips.

"With your brother not available for Thanksgiving, when do I meet your parents again, babe?"

"This Thursday," she whimpered. "Thanksgiving. That hasn't changed."

Kissing her neck, he grumbled. "It's way too long."

"Let me get you a drink, it might help with waiting."

He chuckled. "Drinking you is what I need."

Tapping his cheek, she slowly strolled out of his arms. Reluctant to let her go, he slid one arm around her belly from the side and pulled her back.

A light giggle lit her face. "You're so naughty."

And he tucked his bearded chin at the back of her neck and pasted kisses down her back.

Caught in the trend of his caresses, she pressed back against him. In that position, she did not miss the throbbing of his hard length against her thighs. While she ached with need, his palms trailed upward from behind and sculpted her boobs. Without a bra to hinder his reach, his fingers rolled around her nipples until they cried for pleasure.

Letting out a long moan, she twisted around in his arms, her breath hitched in her throat. His mouth claimed hers in the most heartrate elevating kiss of her life.

Chapter 18 – Makes Me Laugh

Kiarra

"*So*, what was the first thing that struck you about my sister, Kiarra apart from the fact she's beautiful?" Deiondre fired the moment everyone had drinks in their hands at the mini Thanksgiving Dinner put together by Jalicia.

Dressed like a power couple to impress, Kiarra and Ryder arrived in Atlanta Georgia a few hours ago. The engaged duo stepped inside Deiondre's house less than thirty minutes ago. While her older sister had been ecstatic at the opportunity to meet and, to get to know Ryder, her brother had been on the fence.

At the moment they were seated on the taupe L-shaped corner couch in Deiondre's beige-and-grey themed living room. Kiarra, fitted in a sassy and sweet red dress, had her arm linked through Ryder's to offer needed support. She hoped her siblings would not give her fiancé a tough time.

Ryder, arrayed in a knock out two-piece slim-fit black suit and a blue shirt, gave Kiarra a quick, I-got-this glance before addressing her brother's question.

"It was her guts. Kiarra's bold, confident, direct. She unnerved me a little at the time, and I pushed back," Ryder admitted, not holding back.

Kiarra chuckled, nudging her fiancé's side. "Come on, you pushed back a lot."

"What do you mean by you *pushed back*?" Jalicia asked, her light brown eyes turned wary.

Ryder swallowed and raised his free hand.

"I gave Kiarra a hard time at the start."

Jalicia and Deiondre's eyes widened with interest.

"In what way? We're curious," her sister voiced.

Ryder gave a remorseful grin before he said. "I told her I didn't want anything to do with her."

While Jalicia and Kiarra laughed, Deiondre's dark eyes stared into Ryder's hazel pair across the sofa as if he wanted to harm him.

"What changed your mind?" her brother posted in a brisk tone, his expression unreadable now.

"As I got to know Kiarra, I found she had a generous heart, a very loving one. She was there for me in my dark times and she waited patiently for me to get to know her while also gently pushing me out of my gloomy days." Ryder tipped his head to stare at Kiarra before he continued. "I've never met any woman as great as Kiarra. She makes me laugh, whip my ass in line, pardon my language and she loves me unconditionally. So, I fell for her, hard."

Tears pricked the back of Kiarra's eyes. And Jalicia's round face sobered up, but her lips formed into a sweet smile.

"Kiarra's not perfect, I know that. Do you know her flaws?" Her sister perked up.

Ryder grinned and gave Kiarra a side glance before responding.

"No one is perfect. I know I'm not. She put up with my bad side. Kiarra nagged me a lot in the beginning, and she pushes hard sometimes. I found that annoying when I first met her, but I've realized her heart is in a good place and it's because she loves me. She's not that way with other guys."

"Sounds about right," Deiondre and Jalicia admitted with a slow head shake.

"Are you two saying I nag you a lot?" Kiarra slanted her head in her sibling's direction.

"Umm...yes!" Deiondre nodded. "Can be annoying."

Jalicia laughed. "With love, always with love."

"True," her brother agreed with a grin for Kiarra, before he turned to Ryder. "You were saying?"

"I also know Kiarra doesn't like takeaway food, and she can be overbearing about that," her fiancé added.

"That's true," Deiondre nodded. "Okay, so you think you know what you're getting yourself into, Ryder?"

Kiarra croaked and did an elaborate eye roll. "That's not funny, De." She was a little pissed at her brother. Was he trying to sell her short with that last remark?

"Do you have any dark fears about getting married?" Jalicia asked Ryder, so Deiondre did not have to answer to Kiarra's remark.

Ryder did not seem put off anyhow as he replied.

"Before I met Kiarra, I'd dark fears about marriage because of my parents' divorce. Then again, my mom and dad already drifted apart long before the divorce happened. I didn't I want marriage at all. But getting to know Kiarra changed all that. She's taught me many things. I believe ours will be different because we're responsible for our marriage and nobody else's."

Deiondre and Jalicia nodded in agreement.

Kiarra could not have been prouder. Her fiancé was slaying the questions, answering from the depth of his heart. She felt his love and emotion pour out as he spoke. And she hoped her siblings could see what she saw in him. In truth, she needed their acceptance of her relationship with Ryder.

"I'm throwing the same question to you, baby sister." Deiondre directed his gaze to Kiarra's.

"My dark fear is getting married and ending up with a bad marriage. That was my fear before I met Ryder. With him, those dreadful thoughts are absent. I've seen him at his worst, trust me. And I still love him."

"Are you going to give my sister grief going forward?" Her brother's stare was now on her fiancé.

Ryder did not break his gaze from Deiondre's as he spoke. "Not at all. I love Kiarra with my life. I've never felt this strongly about any woman. She's special and I can't live without her. That's why I asked her to be my wife. When she said yes, it was the best moment ever."

"Kiarra's our baby sister and we want her to be very happy," her brother stressed. "We need assurances that you'll treat her right, every time and she will always come first with you."

Where she sat, Kiarra's heart pounded with love for the man seated beside her, but she also loved her brother and sister for looking out for her.

"It's Thanksgiving, the last Thursday in November this year, I give you my word that Kiarra will always come first in my life. She means everything to me. I'll love her with everything in me and with all I have. I know you're a close family and I appreciate that. But your approval means the world to me and Kiarra."

Deiondre looked to Jalicia.

Her older sister exhaled. "I like you already, Ryder. I think you're genuine. My baby sister obviously loves you. All we ask is for you to make her happy all the time. We love her so much and would hate to see dark circles around her eyes."

Everyone laughed.

"We don't want scrapes on her lovely skin." That was her brother adding his own spin. "No secret tears from my sister, Ryder Blade. You're good looking. How do we know you won't cheat on Kiarra?"

"Because I don't want any other woman, not in my life and definitely not in my bed. Kiarra's the best thing that has happened to me. I could never lay a finger on her and, I won't make her miserable."

"Great," Jalicia nodded. "What about your family? How do we know you'll always protect my sister?"

"Kiarra reconciled me and my mom after nearly two decades of family feud. My mom, Lindsay and my sister, Alana love her already. There's no way I'm going to mess this up by God's grace."

Kiarra felt an emotional tug in her heart. She reached one hand to her fiancé's face, pulled his head down and kissed his lips.

"I love you," she whispered for his ears only.

"My love for you is unshakeable," he whispered in return, throwing her a precious grin.

Deiondre cleared his throat. "I want to have a word with Kiarra."

Ryder nodded and removed his hand from Kiarra's. She gave her fiancé a cheering wink before she stood up and followed her brother to the kitchen. While in the kitchen, Deiondre leaned against the double-door fridge and stared at her, his smile full blown now.

Kiarra moved forward and opened her arms. Her brother gave her a bear hug and pecked her cheeks.

"I love you, Kiarra. I don't want to see you hurt."

She nodded. "I know that, De. Ryder's not going to hurt me. I feel it in my heart."

"Tell me, why do you want to marry him?"

"Ryder's got a great heart and he's a big romantic. He doesn't show off. And, he makes me laugh. Most importantly, he gets me. Ryder doesn't complain about my weight, or the size of my legs. I feel amazing when I'm with him. I love him. I loved him from the start and it has only deepened since we got together."

Deiondre wiggled one eyebrow. "Does Ryder have any flaws? He almost sounds too perfect."

Kiarra chuckled. "Not at all. He's not perfect. But I know his flaws and I love him with his good and his bad. That's what makes this a beautiful relationship."

"I see that he's into you. I like the way he looks at you. That's a good thing. You can't fake that. I see how you look at him. You love each other. But what about the prison thing you mentioned on one of our phone conversations?"

She was happy, Deiondre could see that Ryder's love for her was the real thing.

"Ryder made a mistake when he was young, you know like many young people do. He paid for his mistakes and that's it. He built *Rich Earth Coffee* from the ground up. He's done very well for himself and turned his life around. I'm proud of him."

"And you're sure he doesn't do drugs no more?"

"He never did drugs, De. That was his friend. It was a one-time stupid teens mistake."

"OK. Just asking, Ki. What about his values? Do they align with yours? Is he a Christian? Have you talked about how you'll raise your kids? Some white folks never said, Halleluyah once in their whole lives."

"Ryder's got moral values. He wasn't raised a Christian. But he knows my faith is important to me. We've talked about it. His mom has found the Lord. In fact, Ryder goes with me to church and he's open to becoming a Christian. We're going to raise our kids as Christians and in the church."

"Is that what you want, or what you both want? He's going to be the head of the house, Ki. What he says is what's going to happen. I need to be sure you're on the same page."

"We're on the same page, De."

"I want to find out for myself, Ki. No matter how common failed marriages are in this country, divorce is something we don't want in our family. Now is the time to ask all the tough questions. The moment he puts a wedding band on your pretty finger, it's done."

"I got you. Everything will be fine by God's grace."

"Okay. Let's go talk to him some more."

"Don't give him a hard time, De. He wants you to like him. Seriously."

Chuckling, her brother tapped her nose. "That's a good thing."

"What is?"

Her brother threw one hand across her shoulder.

"The fact he cares what I think and wants us to get along. It means he loves you enough to want a united family. Some guys don't give a damn."

"Yeah." She flung one hand around his waist.

When they returned to the living room, Deiondre sat again on the lounge armchair he vacated earlier while Kiarra sat beside Ryder, rubbing his arm. Jalicia stopped talking with Ryder when they re-joined.

"A few more questions, Ryder," Deiondre spoke up, his expression not as sombre as it had been earlier.

Ryder made eye contact with Deiondre.

"Ask away," her fiancé encouraged with a grin.

"My sister told me about your time in prison."

Ryder's fingers stiffened around Kiarra's.

Worried her boyfriend would go on the defensive, Kiarra caressed the back of his hand to assure him everything was okay.

"I know you've done well for yourself as the CEO of *Rich Earth Coffee*. What I want to know is have you done drugs of any type since you got out of prison?"

"No. I never did drugs. I don't take drugs and I don't deal. That's the whole truth."

Deiondre nodded. "Thank you. I know it's a tough question, but if I'm going to say yes to you marrying my sister, I've got to know she's in safe hands."

Her brother's fear was valid. Detroit and other cities were littered with single moms raising kids by themselves because their husbands were too busy committing heinous crimes and getting their asses thrown into prison for long sentences.

"I've got nothing to hide. I'm clean, I want a great life with Kiarra. And I know we'll be happy together."

"Thank you, Ryder for being open with us. Let's talk about faith," her sister initiated with a smile.

Deiondre and Jalicia exchanged a quick look. They might have discussed that prior to meeting, Ryder.

"Kiarra's a Christian, you're not. How's that going to work when you have kids?" Jalicia continued.

"We've talked about this," Ryder responded.

Kiarra gave him a big tick for his first reply.

"When I first met your sister, I'd no faith. I wasn't raised with any. But after I met, Kiarra and I saw her good heart and all she did for me without judging me,

I realized I wanted to learn from her. So, to answer your question, I'm going to be a Christian. And we've agreed we're raising our kids as Christians."

"Great!" her siblings chorused with a clap.

"Let's drink to that," Deiondre said, raising his glass, a warm grin marked his hard features.

Everyone raised their glasses.

"To Kiarra and Ryder. I wish you two a happy and prosperous marriage!" Deiondre cheered to the engaged couple's relief.

"To Kiarra and Ryder. I wish you an adventurous and love-filled married life!" Jalicia laughed a lot.

They all clinked glasses with each other.

Joy spread across Kiarra's face. She giggled, curling one hand around her grinning fiancé. *Lord.* She let out a long breath she did not even know she had trapped in her lungs. She sagged against Ryder and he hugged her tight and pressed his lips on top of hers.

"Thank you," Ryder said to Deiondre, then he directed his eyes to Jalicia. "Thank you for welcoming and accepting me into your family. I won't take your trust for granted."

Ryder extended his hand to Deiondre for a handshake but her brother tugged him forward with one hand. They bumped their shoulders and laughed.

"Take great care of my sister," her older brother said. "Or I'll come after you."

"I'll drop in to see you guys in San Diego on one of my trips," her sister promised. "Ryder, you've got to meet my husband, Leron before the wedding."

Ryder nodded. "I'm in. We can make that happen."

"Speaking about weddings. Do you have a date?" Jalicia asked. "I've got to save the date now."

Kiarra was back in her boyfriend's arms. Sloping her head, she murmured, winking at him.

"Do we have a date, Ryder?"

"We do, babe. Next week."

Deiondre and Jalicia huffed, muttering in unison, "*Next week*?" They looked like heart attack victims.

Ryder and Kiarra laughed.

"Not next week," Kiarra spoke up, to save her siblings from dropping dead.

Promptly, their shocked expressions cleared.

"Really? You're playing games with our hearts already, Ryder?" Deiondre asked with a long laugh.

"Let's go have some food," Jalicia said, shaking her head. "I'm very happy for you, Kiarra. When is the wedding?"

"In six weeks," Kiarra answered, hugging her sister.

"Is that the actual date?" Jalicia shifted her gaze to Ryder. "Confirm."

"Yeah," Ryder nodded, grinning wide.

Deiondre got out his phone and pulled up his planner. "What day and date?"

"It's Thursday, December 31st." Kiarra confirmed the details. "I'm looking forward to saying, *I do* on the last day of this year."

Jalicia tapped her phone and noted the date. She sighed. "Thank the Lord, I'm free. Deiondre, when you're getting married, please give me longer notice."

"How long are we talking?" her brother asked, twisting his lips to the side.

"Like three to six months," Jalicia stated, laughing.

"Why do you need half a year's notice?" Deiondre countered, planting one arm along Jalicia's shoulders.

"That's the way it is, De. So, baby sister what's your wedding colour scheme? We need to go talk."

"Yeah," Kiarra said, smiling. "For colour, we want blue and white with a hint of grey."

"Nice combo." Jalicia nodded. "We've got lots to plan for. Guest list and everything. We'll work on it."

"Yeah, Jal." Winking at her brother, Kiarra crowed. "You'll need a plus-one at our wedding, De."

"Don't even start on me, Ki. Let's have something to eat, right?" Deiondre reminded everyone.

"Someone's deflecting the question," Ryder teased.

"I'll work on it," Deiondre assured them, grinning.

"We've got to meet her before the wedding," Jalicia added in a birdlike voice.

"I'm not seeing anyone if that's what you are all asking. And I don't need you lot intervening in my personal life. Don't refer your friends."

They all laughed but with no intention of adhering.

"Did you cook, De?" Kiarra nudged her brother.

Jalicia snickered behind Deiondre's back. "You know that's not possible. De never learnt to cook."

"Do you cook?" Deiondre asked Ryder.

"I'm learning in Kiarra's cooking school."

"You teaching other people how to cook now, Ki?" Deiondre raised both eyebrows high.

"It's private classes just for Ryder." Kiarra winked.

Everyone split their sides as they laughed.

"Something just occurred to me. I'm going to organize a party tagged, get-to-know the Wright and Blade families. We need to meet Ryder's family before the wedding. Don't you all think so?"

"We do," Kiarra and Ryder replied at the same time.

"Great idea." Deiondre gave a thumb up.

Afterward, the weekend with her siblings went smoothly. They got on with Ryder, and Kiarra could not have been happier. Although she had assured Ryder her siblings would accept him, at the time, she'd had no idea they would. If they had distrusted him, she would have been devastated. But with how things turned out she felt blessed and eager about the future.

While they sat to eat, mac 'n' cheese with steam collard greens, potato salad, coleslaw, steak and sweet potato fries, Kiarra and Ryder stole surreptitious glances and brushed their thighs under the table.

On their way back to San Diego on Saturday, the giddy couple kissed and held hands as they rehashed every question Ryder had been asked by her siblings.

"There's nothing I want more than to have your fingers thread mine and have you look into my eyes for eternity," Kiarra murmured, her gave upturned.

"Kia, what I want most is to brush my mouth over yours and to slide my tongue between your lips to taste your essence forever."

Breathing raggedly, her fiancé skewed his head, slid his tongue between her lips, past her teeth and skated with her tongue from side to side.

A happy-ever-after feeling of love spread through her body and she knew her future with Ryder Blade would remain bright and blessed.

Chapter 19 – Can't Wait

Ryder

Weeks after their engagement, Ryder had his arms around his fiancée's waist while they frolicked in the hot tub at a private beach off the coast of San Diego. Inside the hot water bubbling up to their chests, they linked their legs. Two almost-empty wineglasses and half-eaten snack tray sat on top of a table beside the tub.

"How are you feeling about marrying me?" Ryder recalled the question his fiancée's parents asked last week when he went with her to visit them in Detroit.

Kiarra giggled, wiping water splashes from her face.

"Sounds like you're quoting my dad. Last weekend's visit to my parents was fun. My parents like you."

He chuckled, stroking her thighs stretched across his legs. "I know for a fact your mama likes me. She kept giving me that take-care-of-my-baby-girl glances I liked."

Under the open air, Kiarra's eyes twinkled as she carried on laughing. "Oh! Did I miss those sneaky exchanges then?"

"How could you? It was across the dinner table."

"And what was your response again?"

Winking, he threw her a dirty shrug. "I made her a genuine promise to love and care for you."

"Mm-hmm. In words, or as a silent glance?"

"Both. Your mama pulled me aside to chat."

"Aww. How did I miss that?"

The warm wind rustled between the garden trees bordering the hot tub.

"When you went off with your dad to talk about me, probably."

"That's why I missed it. Mama's chill. Dad's cool."

"When your dad asked why I thought I was the man for you, I think my brain froze for like two seconds."

She laughed, swinging her legs to stand in the tub. "What? I don't believe you. I thought you did great."

"Not for the first few seconds. He gave me that laser gaze that said clearly, lie-to-me-and-I'll-know."

Lying on her belly now, she stretched out her hands and floated toward him. He grasped her fingers and slowly pulled her along until he linked his arms behind her upper back.

"My dad was a little reserved, that's all."

"You think? I thought your dad was hard on me. His questions came thick and fast."

Fluttering her lashes, she arched her neck. "Aww."

In that moment, she looked so damn hot! The woman took his breath away with one glance. With her curvy figure plastered against his in the hot tub now, he wondered how long he could hold back.

"But you held your own, giving him honest and open answers. I was very proud of you like I was when you met Deiondre and Jalicia."

"How proud?" Her praise meant everything to him.

"Very." She winked, pouting her lips.

He laughed, trapped her face between his palms and licked her lips before exploring the inside sweetness of her mouth with his tongue.

"Ready to be my wife?"

"No."

"What?" He frowned.

She giggled, teasing his top lip with her fingers. "I'm looking forward to doing things I've only ever imagined since I first asked you to marry me."

The pinch in his chest cleared. "Like what?"

"Like having four kids for you."

Quickly, his chest filled with inestimable happiness. It was not what he thought she would say.

"Four kids?" At the start, he never imagined he would have any. "I was thinking of maybe one?"

Kiarra wiped off the crease on his brow with her lips. "One? That won't work, Mr. Ryder Blade. Our child would be lonely. It would be unfair and unjust."

Laughing, he nodded. "I get the picture. Two then?"

"Are you going to be the pregnant one? Why do you get to say how many kids my body should carry?"

Locking his hands around her hips, he kissed her nose. "Because I'm going to be with you, experiencing all the discomforts and joys of pregnancy. I've been reading about how talking to the baby in the womb helps the baby's mental development."

Her deep brown eyes flashed with arousal he could tell.

"You sound very sexy right now. Talking about being a dad suits you like a second skin."

He wiggled his brows. "You think?"

"I imagine, yes."

"I intend to be a husband you'll be proud of, Kia."

"Nothing is going to get in the way of that by God's grace. I know."

"Why are you so good to me, Kiarra Wright?"

"Because I love you, Ryder Blade."

He pleated his arms around her and she sat astride him in the hot tub. As she pressed forward, her knees scraped the tub, so she dropped her legs.

"Will you move to *Oceanfront Walk* with me? It's a bigger place. Six bedrooms, six bathrooms, an outdoor pool and with ample room for study and games across three floors. Sea view is great. You could finish that book you talked about when we first met. But without me as the villain."

Laughing, she tilted her head and nipped his neck with her teeth. "I've been so busy running around with you, I've not developed your character enough to kill it like I promised."

A wild buzz surged around his chest. "Then don't."

"I'll move in. Our condos aren't suited for raising a family. Wait, you abandoned your mansion with sea views to join us in the condo without a coastline?"

"When there's no one that matters to share it with, you don't even see the sea, trust me." Waking up everyday was a chore. Now everything was different.

She crinkled her nose and brushed her boobs along his bicep as she reached for the wine glass.

His gut constricted.

"Quick question," Kiarra said after she took a sip.

"What is it?" He collected the glass from her hand, emptied the content inside his mouth and refilled it.

"Why didn't you tell me you owned a home at *Oceanfront Walk* from the onset? I was going to kill you when you opened up to my parents. It was the first time I heard about it. Then, I thought if I killed you, who would I marry?"

Instead of diving into a lengthy explanation he made a chortling sound.

"Wipe that smirk from your handsome face!" she pulled his cheeks. "You've been a very bad boy."

After she released his cheeks, he kissed her sassy lips. Whenever she opened her mouth, all he wanted to do was shut her up with a kiss because they looked great and tasted delicious.

"I'm terrible at giving up information about myself. But I'm relieved you decided not to kill me because you mean everything to me. I wanted to surprise you with the news in my own time."

She kissed the shaped beard under his bottom lip.

"Are there any other surprises I need to know?"

"Like what?" He dipped his head, so she had access.

"Like have you had sex with anyone who works for you? Have you been married before?"

"No to both questions. This is one time I'm grateful I didn't cross those two lines."

She sighed. "Phew! I would've shipped your hard butt back to Colorado!"

He shuddered with laughter at her pronounced southern accent she turned on just for effect. While he did, she floated away.

"I like it when you speak like that, Kia."

"If you're not married, or been married before and you've not had sex with your co-workers, I can forgive anything else, I guess."

"Good. Because I've got a surprise for you."

"Really?" She pulled up the straps of her bath suit.

Licking his lips, he leaned over the side of the tub, got out a key and dangled it in her face.

Eyes wide with shock, she floated back to him and belted his hips with one hand. "What's the key for?"

Looking down, he opened her other palm and pushed the key on to her hand.

Scanning the key with curious eyes, she gasped when she saw the brand name engraved on it.

"Mercedes!" she squealed. "Ryder!"

Kiarra jumped on him pushing her boobs against his chest in a flush embrace.

"That's your pre-wedding gift, a 2019 Mercedes AMG C Class Coupe," he told her, trying to cut his thoughts from the flame tightening his groin.

Giggling, she shook her head. Wet hair loosening from her bun wisped around her neck. His fiancée was everything he had wished for and a whole lot more.

"You can't be serious, Ryder!"

Hooking her hands around his neck, she carried on squealing.

"It's yours, babe." He slinked back her wispy curls with his fingers. "I love you more than anything in this world. Your comfort is what I want. Besides, you put up with my bad attitude, I needed to give you something back."

"I'm marrying you already," his girlfriend gushed.

"Yeah, and that too."

He angled his head and caressed the bridge of her nose with his lips, trailing down the length of her nose and ending on her top lip.

"Thank you so much for the car. I'm Looking forward to our wedding day and to our married life. Living every day without you is like suffering."

Good Lord! His pulse picked up. Palming the side of her face, he breathed on her face before tightening his mouth over hers while he cupped one breast with his other hand.

"Ryder..." Kiarra groaned.

He grunted in return as a fiery buzz surged south in his body. Overheated by her pliant body lapping against his, he tweaked her nipple through her bathing suit and dropped his hand to her hips. Kiarra pushed against him and her fingers drove passion through every length of his back and butt. He drifted his hand to her butt cheeks and pushed her forward until he thought he would die from dry pleasure.

Wild whimpers rushed out of her softly parted lips. Her breathing quickened. Breathing shallow himself, he ground his erection against her thigh while he kneaded her thickened nipple and soon, he heard her loud moan above his growl. Together, they succumbed to the overriding desire that tore their control apart.

Vibrating, he released but not inside her as he would have loved. Thick fluid sipped down his legs and got washed away by the bubbling hot liquid. He wrapped his arms around her passion weakened body. Struggling to stand upright, he shifted back and sat on the inside ledge, carrying her to sit on him.

His fiancée set her face on his shoulder. He was not sure if she had averted her gaze because she was pissed at him.

"Are you okay, Kia?" he whispered, dropping a soft kiss on her temple and drawing a line to her earlobe. "Did I go too far? I know we wanted to wait till after the wedding."

She trembled, slanting her neck.

"Never had a hot tub orgasm before," she mumbled, pressing her lips to his shoulder.

He freed the worry sigh trapped in his gut.

"For a minute there I thought you were upset with me for stepping out of line."

She lifted her head in leisurely. Her eyes still dimmed with craving. "I was a little embarrassed until I realized I wasn't the only one who lost the battle to stay strong."

"Trust me, I tried, but I guess I was too attracted to you to keep it together today, babe."

Leaning his head forward, he caught her nape in one hand, brushed his lips along her bottom lip and placed her hand on the left side of his chest.

"My heart is still pounding for you and always will. I love you, Kia. And I'm going to wait till our wedding night to slide inside you. That's a promise."

"Might as well get married in a hurry because my booty can't wait that long."

He laughed, pulling her into his arms for the hottest hug of his life.

Mini Character Interviews

Dear Reader, here's another chance to get to know more my characters in this mini interview set up by an online magazine called *Inside You*:

◇ ◇ ◇◇ ◇ ◇ ◇ ◇◇ ◇ ◇ ◇

Character Name: Ryder Blade

Ques: Ryder, why did you give Kiarra such a hard time when you first met at the barbecue party?

Ans: {He chuckles} I guess I'm never going to live this one down. Listen, my fiancée came at me strong. I was like, wow, I'm not interested, but the truth was she stirred something hot and strong inside me and that made me jumpy.

Ques: Shouldn't you have been nicer instead?

Ans: Yes, if I'd been ready for that. At the time, my head was all over the place. My emotion was all twisted. But Kiarra helped straighten me out quick.

Ques: You kept many details about yourself from Kiarra. Why?

Ans: As the CEO of a successful business, women with dubious intentions and appeal are attracted to me. I got sick of that lifestyle. When I met Kiarra, I was in hiding I would say, so she got the wrong end of the stick for reasons that had nothing to do with her. I've apologized for not being upfront with Kiarra.

Ques: When did you know Kiarra was the one?

Ans: The day she made me pancakes in my condo. Everything suddenly clicked. It all fell into place. I just knew in my heart she was the one.

Ques: *Because she made it like your mom?*

Ans: Partly. That scene took me back to a time in my life when I was happiest, before all the chaos of my parents' separation and divorce, feeling abandoned by my mom and my detachment issues.

Ques: *Do you still feel guilty for how mean you were to Kiarra before you realized she was the one?*

Ans: Not anymore. Kiarra forgave me. I've worked through my issues. Now I've got my whole life to prove to Kiarra how much I love her.

Ques: *Ryder, because of the timing did you think Kiarra would accept your marriage proposal?*

Ans: During our break up, I prayed like I've never done. I went to church at odd hours just praying for her to have me back. I couldn't really sleep, or eat. Kiarra's my world. She makes me laugh. She brings life to simple things. Cooking is fun with her, you know, so not having her with me was horrible. To answer your question, the answer is no, I wasn't sure she would say yes. But I'd intended to show her that I was a different guy.

Ques: *How did you feel when she said yes?*

Ans: Before that, Kiarra told me she loved me the moment I walked in through the door. Mind you, this was after our break. I almost couldn't breathe. I was in shock. I immediately went on one knee to ask her to marry me. It was perfect timing. I felt like I'd won a priceless gift from God. I was more than happy. I can say I felt like my life was about to start for good and greatness was now achievable with Kiarra by my side.

Ques: *What great things do you hope achieve?*

Ans: Many. Getting married to Kiarra is top on the list. Having two kids with her follows closely. Others would be making Kiarra fall in love with me every day while I grow *Rich Earth Coffee* empire across the pond to Europe and even to Australia as a legacy for our children. Lastly, growing old with Kiarra.

Ques: *Awesome! What advise do you have for single women looking to date a guy they fancy?*

Ans: {Ryder grins} I'd say use Kiarra's tactics. If she hadn't pushed hard, I may not have seen what was right in front of me. Sometimes, women think every guy wants to get in their pants. It's not always true. Depending on what's going on inside his head, or in his life, he may not even see you at all. But if you try talking to him, and telling him a few harsh truths, like Kiarra did, he'll take notice for sure.

Ques: *Do you intend to have kids right away?*

Ans: Yes, by God's grace like my fiancée says.

Ques: *Is the gender of the baby important to you?*

Ans: Not at all. I'll be grateful to have a baby boy, or girl with my beautiful wife. Have you seen her eyes and gorgeous curves? That woman takes my breath away. Girl, or boy, I'll be an extremely happy dad.

Ques: *Where are you going for your honeymoon?*

Ans: Somewhere warm for sure. Look out, you'll find out in due time.

Ques: *The readers are curious to know, Ryder.*

Ans: OK. We're off to *Stella Island*.

Ques: *Stella Island? Where's that?*

Ans: There you go. My fiancée mentioned it in passing. That's why my gorgeous queen is getting her dream honeymoon destination. The setting will blow anyone's mind away.

Ques: *Ryder, thank you for your time with Inside You. We hope you have a blissful married life.*

Ans: Thank you for having me.

◇ ◇ ◇ ◇◇ ◇ ◇ ◇◇ ◇ ◇ ◇

Character Name: Kiarra Wright

Ques: Every black sister wants to know where you found the guts to go for a sexy guy you fancied?

Ans: {Kiarra laughs} Frankly, I'll be lying to you if I said I didn't fancy Ryder at first sight. Have you seen my fiancé? He's gorgeous from head to toe.

Ques: No one will believe you if you denied it.

Ans: {She laughs again} I know. Where did I get the guts? I didn't think before I acted. That's the truth. If I'd stopped to think, I might have changed my mind. Ryder had this dark expression when I first saw him. But I could also see he needed some sort of emotional connection I could share with him.

Ques: What do you mean by when you first saw him? Wasn't the barbecue party the first time you two met?

Ans: {She shook her head} Not for me. I'd seen Ryder twice when he was taking out trash. I was taking out mine when I sighted him. I ducked and watched him. His arm muscles got my pulse racing.

Ques: Wow! You kept that fact to yourself. Does Ryder know?

Ans: Not yet. There'll be time to tell him.

Ques: When did you know Ryder was the one?

Ans: On our first date, inside the helicopter. It just clicked into place. I felt it in my heart, in my soul that I'd met the one. Again, at dinner with his mom and sister, I got clarity. But when we broke up for two weeks after he told me about his past in prison, I knew I couldn't live without it. God bless my mom, she helped me sort out my thoughts. At that point, I knew for a fact I loved him deeply and nothing else mattered.

Ques: *Did you know he was going to propose when he did?*

Ans: Not at all! We'd been on a break. I couldn't sleep. I couldn't eat. I wanted to see him to tell him everything was okay, that his time in prison was in the past and I'm willing to let it remain in the past. I wanted to feel his arms around me again. Truth is I wasn't a hundred percent sure he was going to be waiting for me at the end of two weeks you know. The last thing I thought of was a marriage proposal.

Ques: *Can you describe your feelings to us after he went on one knee. I'm assuming he did.*

Ans: {She giggles} Honestly when he went on one knee after we hugged, my heart exploded with wild joy and a feeling of *I'm finally home.* Sometimes you think some guy is on the same page as you because he says it, but it doesn't work out. When Ryder asked me to marry him along with all the amazing things, he said to me, I wanted to jump high to touch the sky. It was an awesome feeling. Thank God.

Ques: *If you could change one thing about Ryder what will it be?*

Ans: Maybe if his gloomy side stayed hidden? I don't know. I can handle him anyway, so it doesn't matter. I'll say, nothing. I love Ryder the way he is.

Ques: *Was there another reason you didn't take Ryder to meet your parents for Thanksgiving?*

Ans: Yeah. My dad told me the only way he would meet Ryder was if he first met with Deiondre and Jalicia and they approved our relationship.

Ques: *Interesting. What do you look forward to most during your honeymoon?*

Ans: Stretching my naked body along Ryder's, having lots of sex and learning to love him more.

Ques: *Right. Are you planning on having a baby as soon as possible?*

Ans: Only the Lord knows for sure. But Ryder and I, will give it our best shot while having great sex.

Ques: *Sure. If you could change one thing about your dating experience, what will it be?*

Ans: That I'd met Ryder earlier. He makes me so happy. How did I live so long without him?

Ques: *Has Zack finally accepted the fact you've moved on?*

Ans: Ah, yeah. He's going to be at our wedding. Zack met someone new. I'm happy for him.

Ques: *Wow, that's amazing for Zack. We wish you and Ryder a very happy married life.*

Ans: Thank you so much for having me.

◊ ◊ ◊ ◊◊ ◊ ◊ ◊◊ ◊ ◊ ◊

Character Name: Deiondre Wright

Ques: *As a successful black bachelor in Atlanta Georgia, do we expect wedding bells to ring soon?*

Ans: I'm only thirty-three. I've got my life ahead of me. There's no hurry for me to get married.

Ques: *Is that because you've not met the one?*

Ans: That's a huge part of it. With divorce rates climbing up to the sky daily in the US, I've got to be cautious. I don't want to be part of the statistics.

Ques: *That's true. But there are many black sisters out there ready to walk down the aisle with a cute professional like you.*

Ans: {He chuckles} Seriously? Where are these single women? First, you've got to make sure she can dazzle me with her cooking skills. I can boil an egg confidently. That's about it. Second, she got to have respect. Many women don't know the first thing about respect. They hide under the *gender equality* slogan to disrespect their husbands.

Ques: *So, what do you expect married life to be?*

Ans: Happy, peaceful, loving, fun, adventurous. I want to marry my best friend, someone I can share my heart, my fears and my dreams with. I need someone I can love and who loves me back. A woman I can call my equal, but she respects me and I respect her. A woman I'll support and encourage to achieve her dreams. A woman who'll share her insecurities with me and I'll tell her, she's bigger than her flaws. I don't want a woman who cusses for a living, or who spends money like I'm a cash machine.

Ques: *Got the list. Is religion a deal breaker?*

Ans: A big yeah. If she's not a Christian, forget it. I'll not compromise my faith for love. It doesn't work.

Ques: *You're pretty set in the way you think.*

Ans: I know what I want. It's that simple.

Ques: *Are you actively dating?*

Ans: Yes and No.

Ques: *Care to explain?*

Ans: Yes, I date and no, it's not actively. The reason is simple. When I go on a series of dates and I've got to endure strained conversations, or I find I've got nothing in common with her, or all I see are dollar signs in the pair of eyes seated across from me, I wonder why I bothered.

Ques: *Where do you meet these women?*

Ans: Is there a right place?

Ques: *At the Church? Volunteering. Festivals.*

Ans: Volunteering? I didn't think of that. Thanks.

Ques: *Have you tried dating apps?*

Ans: {He throws back his head and laughs} Never.

Ques: You've got something against dating apps?

Ans: I'm not a dating app guy, that's all. I don't want a screen between me and the woman I want to date. I'm a traditionalist in that way.

Ques: We hope you find your soul mate soon and live your happy-ever-after with her.

Ans: I pray so. Thank you for having me

Interviewer: The pleasure is ours at *Inside You Online Magazine*, Deiondre.

Deiondre: Are you married?

Interviewer giggles: Why are you asking?

Deiondre: Like Ryder Blade, I just realized I need to see what's front of me.

Interviewer: I'm single.

Deiondre: Care to have a drink with me sometime?

Interviewer: Let me get back to you on that.

Deiondre: Are you blowing me off?

Interviewer: No. I've got a busy week of interviews for the next week and a half. That's all.

Deiondre: Then let's say we have a drink in two weeks? Saturday, 8p.m. to be exact?

Interviewer: You're a persistent man, Deiondre.

Deiondre: Is that a yes?

Interviewer: {After a pause, she nods} Yes.

Deiondre: Great. I look forward to it. Your name is?

Interviewer: Teona Lewis

Deiondre: Teona. That's a beautiful name. It was a real pleasure to meet you, Teona. See you soon.

Interviewer: Same here. Thank you. Take care of yourself, Deiondre.

Deiondre: Will do.

◇ ◇ ◇ ◇◇ ◇ ◇ ◇◇ ◇ ◇ ◇

Character Name: Jalicia Jackson

Ques: What grade do you teach, Jalicia?

Ans: Junior high.

Ques: Whoa! How long have you been a high school teacher in New Jersey?

Ans: It's been six good years with steady progress.

Ques: Do you plan to have kids sometime?

Ans: Yeah. When we first got married, Leron and I agreed to focus on our careers first. Now that's done, we're going to start trying for a baby, by God's grace.

Ques: How important is the sex of the baby?

Ans: Well, a baby girl would be adorable to me. But Leron wants an NFL star baby boy.

Ques: Exciting. Do you feel if you'd taken time off to have a baby, it might have hurt your career?

Ans: That thought occurred to me when I first got married, it's the reason we waited. It was important to me to establish myself as a high-performing high school teacher before starting a family.

Interviewer: We wish you continued happiness and a blissful life full of kids with Leron.

Jalicia: Thank you very much. I wish you the same.

Interviewer: That's kind of you. Thank you, Jalicia.

◇ ◇ ◇ ◇◇ ◇ ◇ ◇◇ ◇ ◇ ◇

Chapter 20 – Come All Over

Stella Island

Kiarra

After their lovely wedding ceremony at *New Providence Baptist Church* in Detroit, Michigan attended by all their family members, friends and selected colleagues, Kiarra and Ryder Blade flew to *Stella Island* for their honeymoon.

Situated in the Greek Island of *Crete*, the glistening blue waters and pristine white sand surrounding the resort, *Stella Luxury Suites & Spa* welcomed the honeymooners to an absolutely incredible, sunny and serene destination.

"I love this place," Kiarra gushed once they entered their overwater bungalow. Giggling, she removed her sunglasses, marvelling at nature's beauty. "There's sparkling blue water everywhere. When I revealed to you, *Stella Island* was my number one place in the world to see, I never imagined you'll fly me here."

Hanging his sunglasses on his head, a laughing Ryder wrapped his arms around her from behind. "Anything for you, babe. You're my queen. I also love it here. Refreshing cool air. Want a drink?"

"Water please, my gorgeous husband."

"Sounds perfect." Chuckling, he kissed her earlobe.

"What else is perfect, honey?"

One tremor stiffened her nipples. The thought of his length sliding inside her softness sent liquid spilling into her red lace panties. From where she stood by the floor-to-window sliding glass doors, she observed her husband pour two glasses of water. Magnificent in body and in his flawed character, she felt truly blessed to be married to Ryder Blade.

Swallowing the gap between them with his long strides, Ryder handed her one glass of water and also immediately ordered champagne and a four-course dinner to be delivered in an hour.

"Why an hour?" She winked while drinking the cold water that quenched her thirst just right.

"Because I've got some business to take care of," he said in the same deep voice she fell for from day one.

Feeling the sizzling vibes from his swagger, she stroked his chest with her eyes.

Ryder took a few steps closer. Inside her chest, her heart leaped. This was the moment she had longed for from the day he asked her on their first date. She did not want to waste an extra minute waiting.

"What were you thinking when you put on this sexy crisscross front dress–" he spooled his fingers around the crisscross design at the front of her dress.

Warm bubbles expanded inside her boobs already.

"–with the lace up at the side to reveal your thigh?" His left fingers lifted her red and gold ruched party dress to caress her thigh working up to her butt cheek.

She shuddered as a million quakes split through her body. Moans of different sizes launched out of her mouth. So, she steadied herself by throwing her hands around his waist. *Damn!* His muscles, dense and hot filled her fingers with electric bolts. She rolled her palms around every ridge and curve of muscle from his shoulder down to his butt cheeks.

In the same vein, her husband squeezed her ass so tight, she clenched her inner muscles. Her pulse rate elevated fast, she had to take in a sharp inhale.

"Don't think I can wait, honey. Get inside me," she moaned, throwing her resistance to the white sand.

"You've got to wait, Kia," he crooned, nipping her neck, brushing his lips along her shoulders while he slid one hand around her hips to cup her mound.

"Ah!" she crowed, as hot liquid dripped. She could feel it. Her heart beat so fast, she could not breathe.

"Ryder, slide inside me now!" She shut her eyes, and threw her head back, giving in to the slow burning pleasure surging up to her cleavage.

"Sliding inside you is one of my goals." His words were uttered in a low, body-tingling whisper.

Releasing her for a second, he grabbed the hem of her knee-length dress and pulled it over her head. Opening her eyes, she did the same for his dark shirt and immediately unbuttoned his tailored pants. Ryder, also eager, stepped out of his clothes.

It felt amazing to stand almost nude in front of him. She had thought she would be shy, or insecure.

His gorgeous eyes roamed around her face, grew wide as they dipped to her boobs cocooned in a bra one size smaller before lowering to her thighs. Letting out a shallow exhale, Ryder touched her shoulders with reverence while his fingers undid her bra.

When her boobs jumped out of her flirty underwired plunge lace bra, he discarded it over his head. His eyes darkened and his jaw tightened.

"My God, your beauty is excellent, Kiarra Blade."

His words were followed by a grunt.

"With compliments like that, can my head get any bigger?" Relieved he loved the sight of her heavy boobs, she carried on shaping his perfect abs with her ready hands.

"You're very stunning, my Kia," he paired his words with soft tweaks of her nipples with both hands.

Arching her back, she whimpered as tingling feelings coursed through her cleavage. Heat blew into a slow flame across her body. It felt so good.

"I'm ready for you." She let out a long exhale. "I need you inside me." Her chest felt like it would burst with pleasure, yet he had not even slid inside.

"I want you more, Kia," he whispered, crushing his mouth over hers in a masterful kiss.

Thunder bolts hit her body from every angle. She kissed him back with hunger, with greed and with a longing so strong, she wanted to cry out. She snaked her fingers all over his body in no particular order. All she needed now was to feel his skin against hers and for his erection to stretch her wet inside as wide as possible.

With one hand, her husband packed her butt cheeks and jerked her hips forward. Purring, she lowered her right hand from his abs. Lord, his chiselled muscles were a wonderful delight for her hands. Across the dips and rise of his rigid six-pack, her fingers flowed again. Eager to delve down, she drifted her hands to his crotch.

Ryder grunted inside her mouth.

Her heart hopped with a burning longing.

The soft hair around his erection teased her fingers. Swirling her tongue inside Ryder's mouth, she wound her fingers around his hardened length. She gasped. Warmth burned her fingers. His thickness and length kicked her heat level outside the chart. And Ryder swept his lips to the corner of her mouth, his grunt deepening to her satisfaction.

"Ow. Feels great, babe."

"Want some more?" She moved her hand along his shaft and squeezed a little and then harder.

He jerked against her, squeezed her butt cheeks and bent his head to hose her nipple with his hot mouth. She moaned as many stars erupted at the back of her eyes. Quickly, he moved one hand to lift her breast while he sucked and teased her nipple.

Lost in a world of feral desire, she groaned. If he did not slide inside her now, she would lose her mind. The heat burning her cleavage was fierce.

"Your breast tastes like the best champagne in the world." He pulled his other hand around to massage her soft folds.

A great wave of enjoyment hit her inside. Moaning, she jerked against his hand and totally forgot to tease his erection. Before she could put her thoughts together, her husband swept her off her feet after he peeled off his cotton stretch boxer.

Filled with raging passion, she circled her legs around his waist, or tried to like they did in the movies. But her not-so-long, thick legs dropped. Ryder aided her legs up with solid strong arms.

She wound her arms around his neck and kissed his lips, while he slid his pounding hardened length inside her pulsing wetness.

Savage flames trolled inside her as a feeling of intense fullness filled her body. It felt right. Perfect. Like she was truly home.

A deep-throated rumble gushed out of Ryder's lips. "You're freaking hot, Kia! So wet for me."

This was what she had longed for since they started dating. He pushed her hips forward with both hands and she jerked against him to deepen the sexual ride. Ryder, stronger than the best stallion rode her the way she needed to be entertained.

"Hard as rock, you fill me perfectly," she sobbed.

A sense of euphoria enveloped her senses. Scorching sensations somersaulted between her thighs, shot up to her belly and scalded her cleavage.

They both cried out with a passion so great, she almost felt the ground shudder.

The initial rush of warmth and fullness got her blood pumping and heart racing.

"You're fucking delicious, Kia!" her husband raged, plunging deeper and moving his hips with great skill.

"You pound me great, honey!"

She tossed her head back and abandoned any control she ever had. The ferocious sweetness flourished around her outer folds but inside, she was almost exploding with pleasure as his erection found every nook and cranny.

"Do I?" he grunted, kissing her neck. "Say it again."

Kiarra could only moan in response as a wind storm hit her body. Forward, backward, she hit her hips, as waves of electricity coursed through her. Her face and body warmed up like she was lying on a stove.

Ryder bowed his head, trapped her other nipple with his mouth and plunged his erection so deep inside her, she shrieked with gratification. Pressure assembled inside her with every passing second. His erection sprang back and forth. Her inside stretched wider and deeper by his overriding fullness, she felt like she was overheating.

"I'm coming, Ryder!" She gasped.

"Yeah! Come all over my hardness, Kia."

He licked her breast and kneaded her nipple with the edge of his teeth. Indescribable sweetness clogged her insides. Feeling unsteady, she gripped his shoulders tight and rammed her hips against his own. As the pleasure built up faster, Ryder sharpened his thrusts. Intense euphoria rocked her, lifted her to cloud nine and sent her falling in a downward spin.

"Ryder, I'm comi–"

Within seconds, she completely convulsed against him. Around his neck, her hands quivered. Shivers splashed through her body in rivulets.

But he did not wait a heartbeat while she came. Her husband delved his pleasure-giving length inside her, intensifying her pleasure to the point, she could not breathe. In fact, her breaths came out in shallow bursts, she gasped for more air. Her face burned up with heat as she tried to tighten her muscles around his long length.

Moments later, she worked up a little strength to clench her muscles around his energetic erection. His face contorted. She kept up the release and compress motion until the muscles along his neck thickened and stood out.

"Come for me," she whispered in his ear. "I long for you, Ryder."

"Ready, babe?" he ground out through tight lips, his face and neck a brick red hue.

"Come inside my wetness, honey."

"I'm coming, K–" He shut his eyes tight as he jerked forward and stilled, his words cut off by his savage orgasm.

Moved by the sight of him vibrating with love, she caressed the back of his neck and fished her fingers through his hair. Nothing was more satisfying than to receive love and an out-of-this-world sex from the man who was her flawed hero turned husband.

Carrying her in his arms, he strode toward the bed, set her down gently and plugged her swollen lips with a soft peck. "You're freaking amazing, Kia!"

"That was awesome sex, Ryder. Thank you."

Her satiated body welcomed the hardness of her husband's physique. Paired with the softness of the bed, joy in every shade ruptured in her heart.

Once their heart rates climbed back down, she asked. "Did my squishy belly get in the way?"

He wrapped his lips over her mouth and patted her belly. "The only feeling I got when I was inside you was of loving every inch of your tightness. There's nowhere else I wanted to penetrate, except your delicious wetness. My mind zeroed out everything else. But your belly and cellulite added zest to my experience."

She giggled. Cupping his face, she kissed his nose. "I love you more Ryder for being so expressive about your feelings for me."

Grinning, he cupped her butt. "Anytime babe."

With her stomach grumbling now, she pointed at the glass bowl hosting a range of tropical fruits sitting on the wooden sideboard beneath the wall-mounted plasma TV.

"The ripe bananas, oranges, mangoes and uncut pineapple are peeping at me. Should we eat some?"

"Would love to, babe."

Kissing her lips from one side, her husband chuckled. "Was that your belly?"

"Mm-hmm." She giggled. "I'm hungry. The bananas are begging to be eaten."

Totally at home with his body, her husband pecked her shoulder, rolled off the bed and strode toward the sideboard. His naked butt cheeks clenched and relaxed with each step.

Turned on, she whistled. "I like what I see."

He tossed her a hot wink across his shoulder, "My butt, or the banana?"

"Come back to bed and I'll tell you my choice."

Ryder made a U-turn. He stared at his hardening length, groaning. "See what you've done?"

She swirled her tongue along her bottom lip and cuddled one breast. "Don't know what you mean. I asked for a banana."

Growling, he picked up the bunch of ripe bananas, snapped one off, but his eyes never left hers.

"This–," he lifted the banana in one hand, "–or that?" With his free hand, he handled his beautiful hardened erection.

Her boobs gushed with juicy warmth and her nipples peaked again. Moaning, she squeezed her breasts with both hands.

"I want both, Ryder."

"How?"

"The banana in my mouth and your gorgeous length inside me."

Chapter 21 – Between Your Legs

Ryder

A week later, Ryder escorted his wife out to the food hotspot afloat on the outdoor lagoon-like pool on the resort grounds.

"I'm told this restaurant is famed for extravagant Asian cuisine," he informed his wife, dressed in a hot mini black skirt and a sheer flowered top with no sleeves. The morning sunrays kissed her bronzed skin to a glimmering hue, her eyes sparkled and her fingers clung around his waist the way he loved it.

"I like Thai food. But I've not tried Japanese food." Kiarra scrunched her nose. "Should I trust you?"

He coiled one hand around her waist. "Yeah. I hear it's equipped with a modern Robata Grill. I'm pretty sure you can digest the food."

"Ow, isn't that the open charcoal grill thing?"

"Yeah. It's the popular traditional Japanese dining experience. Seafood and vegetables are cooked over an open charcoal grill. You'll love it."

"Welcome to *Umami Asian Robbata*," a waiter–clothed in a modern Japanese styled jacket and pants uniform–greeted with a thin grin.

Once settled, they ordered drinks and food with the added pleasure of watching their meal prepared in the centre of the restaurant. Around them people did their own thing. But he was not interested in anything, or anyone else. Making his wife happy was his singular interest. From the loosely packed tresses framing her neck to her flawless features and delicious curves, she was an epitome of dark beauty.

"Love the way your hair curls around your neck and the sides of your face. It's sexy, Kia."

She giggled, immediately curling her fingers around the dark ends. Her lips parted fully into a magnificent smile, revealing beautiful set of teeth as she leaned forward. Tickled by her boldness, he pressed ahead and caught her lips in a short kiss.

After they were done eating, he took Kiarra's hands across the wooden table and guided her to her feet. Just before they exited their villa earlier, Kiarra had bent over to pick her purse. The curve of her hips got his length tightening in his shorts.

"Thank you for marrying me, Kiarra Blade."

She beamed, and her deep brown eyes reflected love in its purest form. "Do you know at the back of my head I still believe I married you?"

Laughing at her ridiculous assertion, he cuddled her hips and trapped her body within the circle of his hands.

"What gave you such a preposterous idea?" Breathing along her neck, he combed her earlobe with his nose and lips.

His wife squirmed in his arms, pushing her hips along his thigh. Strong heat pooled in his abs, the sound of her giggles a wonderful delight to his ears.

"I asked you to marry me first, didn't I?" she asked when she caught her breath.

Pleating his fingers behind her back, he nodded. "OK. You beat me to it, at first," he agreed, sweeping his tongue between her robust lips to dive inside her mouth. While her fingers teased his skin, her tongue caressed every niche inside his mouth and he felt like he was undergoing an amazing adventure.

"You're the woman of my dreams," he whispered, pressing his lips to the back of her ear.

She shivered, clenching her fingers around his waist. "Hmm... Just keep talking. I don't know what I did before we met, but it dimmed the moment you gripped my heart."

Not done with expressing his feelings, he kissed the column of her neck. "In every way, you're perfect for me, Kia. I've never been happier in my entire life. When I've got my hands wrapped around you, like this and my tongue is nestling between your lush lips, it feels surreal."

Kiarra's eyes bulged, her breathing turned shallow.

"Whoa! Touch my chest–" she purred.

Unwilling to pass up the chance, he placed his left palm over her left breast and squeezed before she completed the invitation.

An immense feeling of pleasure stabbed his arm. It shot up his spine and ended in his groin.

"Yeah. Your heart is rocking," he confirmed, even as warm heat from her full moon breast scorched his hand all the way to his crotch.

Kiarra inhaled and her eyes smouldered.

"People are here, Ryder. And, we've got a date to discover *Crete* today."

"I need somewhere to put my erection first."

"I want you to fill me up too, but–"

Willing to ditch the journey they had already cancelled thrice, he asked. "Crete, or sex?"

"Crete now, sex when we get back."

Groaning in her hair, he cupped her face.

"Only because you're hot and curvy, Kia. Let's go before I change my mind."

With her hand tucked in his own they went on a walk around the island of mythology. Starting at the Fishing Harbour at *Heraklion*, close to *Koules*, they found out it had been used as fortification against intruders for centuries. They also toured *St. Mark's Basilica* now the *Municipal Art Gallery* where they admired arts and crafts exhibitions on display.

For several hours during their trip, they learned about the culture, history and local traditions. In fact, the magnificent landscape of *Stella Island* blew their minds.

Yet, throughout the trip, Kiarra's moans while he entered her tightness kept sneaking in and replaying in his heart. He could even still smell her luxury juice, a major turn on the entire trip.

He was sure his wife did not do any better. Though she insisted on the trip she gave him furtive glances and flirty winks at intervals, mouthing his words, "*I need to put my erection somewhere,*" at one point.

"Next time, I'm going to slide inside your wetness before we go anywhere," he dripped the promise in her ear at the end of the adventure.

Back at the resort later in the day, totally impatient now, he sneaked inside the female toilet after his wife. Before he shut the door, he took a quick look at either side of the hall to check for guests and staff. No one was about. Feeling a rush of pleasure, he turned the lock. From behind, Kiarra hugged him and pressed her face to his back. Aroused already, he turned around, lifted her and carried her to sit on the black marble vanity top. She giggled, pointing at the mirror on the opposite wall.

"What if there's a camera?"

He cupped her mouth with one hand. "Make no sound," he urged, pushing one hand under her skirt.

Nodding, she spread her legs apart. "Taste me," she whispered. "I love it when you stick your tongue inside me."

His chest thundered. To hear his wife say she enjoyed how he loved her, got him so hard, it hurt. "I'm crazy about your tight pussy."

Bending at his waist, he pushed his head inside her short skirt, peeled off her thongs and traced her folds with his fingers first.

A loud moan ran out of her mouth.

Winking, he lifted his head. "Shut it, Kia."

Nodding fast, her eyes fluttered.

"It feels good," she murmured breathing shallow.

With his hard length pulsating between his legs, he fingered her wetness first. Her warm juice left him aching to slide inside her. But he also loved the sexy sounds she made when he tasted her, or plunged his fingers inside her. Desire beat down in his ears. He flicked his tongue across the soft folds while he glided his fingers inside her. Sharp sensations, good in every way gushed through his skin.

Panting, she jerked forward and back repeatedly. Her hands moulded his head as she whimpered softly.

"Ryder-r..."

He smoothened her entrance with his tongue, sucking and taunting. She tasted like an exotic fruit and he could not have enough of her indulgent flavour even if he sucked her all day and night.

"You taste so fucking sweet!" he groaned.

With his wife, sex was exploratory, fun and a nourishment he needed to survive and thrive.

Her thighs pushed against his ear. His groin vibrated with need. Pressing down on her merry spot, he teased and caressed with his tongue and fingers until she balked and jolted, moaning loud. He reached up to her face with one hand and covered her mouth with his palm.

While she came in his mouth, he deepened his fingers inside her and stamped down his tongue. While she quivered, he lifted his head and unzipped his shorts. Just as he was about to slide inside her, Kiarra jumped down from the vanity top and handled his pounding length with both hands and her mouth.

He groaned inwardly as flames scalded his body. Longing to eject, he pumped inside her mouth, grunting as his body ached for her tightness. Her warm mouth was good, but it did not compare with the overwhelming feelings that ravished him whenever he plunged inside her steaming depth.

"I want to come inside you," he pleaded. "Let me slide in, babe."

"One minute," she croaked, sliding her tongue along his shaft and teasing his balls with her lips.

As great as he felt at the moment, her mouth was not deep enough, or wide enough. There was nowhere like her pulsing deepness that embraced his full length to perfection.

He jerked forward. Clamping her shoulders to still her tongue action, he shook her a little.

Licking her lips, she inhaled. "You're so freaking hard and you taste so good."

Gritting his teeth, he lifted her to perch on the end of the vanity top. Without preamble, he lurched inside her and stilled. He groaned as pleasure bourgeoned in his groin spreading up his belly to his chest in mighty ripples. Nowhere else in the world felt like this. Inside Kiarra was home. His erection filled up with deep love and gratitude as her inner soft skin stretched over his stiffness, welcoming him home.

Cupping her ass with both hands, he drove inside her like he wanted to have all of her.

Moaning, Kiarra leaned back on her elbows, pushed her butt forward, so he plunged deeper. Ecstasy surged through him. Left, right, up, down, he banged his wife until his body lost every trace of control. He growled in his gut, clenched his fingers around her naked butt and ground against her.

Wanting more with Kiarra was now a norm. No matter how many times he entered inside her exotic depth, he wanted to go back for more.

Leaning her head back, she convulsed with overriding pleasure while she continued to tighten her muscles around his length. An intense quake blew off the lid on his control switch. Inclining his head to meet Kiarra's, he bumped forward, gripped her hips as he climaxed hard.

She cupped his face, swept her lips over his, muttering, "I love you, Ryder Blade."

"We should do this more often," he whispered in her ear as he cleaned up.

"True. Quickies with you is a wonderful adventure."

On their final week in *Stella Island*, Ryder dived in to the pool surrounding their bungalow on Wednesday afternoon, pulling his wife along despite her squeals of protest.

After convincing her to play sports with him, they had fun playing aqua volleyball for the next half hour. He teased her throughout the game and Kiarra did not hold back throwing dirt as good as she got.

"After all, your hot pink bikini wasn't going to swim by itself," he justified, laughing when she shook out water from her hair at one point.

"You're not getting any sex tonight," she warned, giggling.

"What? I'm in the dog house for getting you to swim and play water volleyball with me?"

He swam across the length of the pool, steering in her direction after several laps.

A few yards from him, Kiarra swam with her head above water at a slower pace.

"Not in the dog house just yet," she clarified. "You'll lie beside me on the bed, but you're not getting any."

"Are you going to be naked?"

Her scowling features faded as she giggled. "Yeah."

"OK then. I can slide in when you're asleep."

The mere thought of that happening got his john thickening fast.

His wife laughed. "Not happening."

"What do I have to do to get some after we're done swimming?"

"You'll wash, condition and dry my hair. Then, you'll massage my feet and—"

He floated to her side and swept his curvy wife into his arms and headed out of the pool. This time she did not protest, curling her arms around his neck instead as a goofy smile appeared on her beautiful oval face.

Chuckling, he kissed her lips. "Have I redeemed myself yet?"

"It's a good start," she mumbled, licking his top lip.

After a short stint in the *Steam Room*, he scrubbed her body with scented body scrub and she rubbed his own with eager hands. On her insistence, he also polished her body with brown sugar body polish. Rinsing off later in the outdoor pool, he was a tad hard. OK. A rock-hard erection was more like it.

"What if I told you I'm hard already, babe?"

"I'll say jump in the cold shower, honey."

"And I'll say you're the most beautiful woman in the world, how can I resist you?"

Kiarra dissolved into lovely giggles.

Too aroused for anymore delay, he ground his mouth across hers and hoisted her across the pool to the private hot tub inside their bungalow. Smiling, she caressed his bottom lip with her tender tongue.

"I love your sexy ass, Kiarra Blade."

"Fuck me, Ryder," she whispered in his ear.

Stimulated to the point of near release, he pinned her inside the hot tub, swept her bikini bottom aside and thrust his erection inside her. Despite the hot water bobbing and bubbling around them, her delicious tight heat enveloped him fully as usual. She wound her arms around his neck and placed smooth kisses along his chest. Taking his nipple inside her mouth, she swiped her tongue across his breast.

Blazes spread along his chest, heading south to his already aching john. He dived inside her deeper, backed out, plunged in again to glimpse the joy caught between her legs. When desire almost overthrew him, he gripped the edge of the hot tub with one hand and clasped her breast with his free hand.

The weight of her breast in his hand was marvellous. It was soft and full, sending whirring heat through his senses.

Kiarra tasted his chest, and shoulders, overheating his skin. Her fingers tore through his hair and across his back. In between, her groans set his senses on fire.

Growling, he drifted one hand to her folds, combed through the thin layer of hair and found her entrance. The second his fingers teased her soft skin, he charged against her back and forth.

Kiarra groaned, gasping as she jerked against his him over and over as she climaxed. He felt her hot juice sear his erection. Nothing in the world compared to the feeling of floating in the sky. The tightening motion of her inner muscles tipped him over. He could not contain the emotional seeds storming through his body as he ejected inside her pulsing heat.

Tossing his head back, he roared. For a few seconds, he stood board-straight. His fingers dug into his wife's hips, as pleasure ripped his body to shreds.

In his ear, Kiarra gave a long, deep moan.

"I loved it, Ryder Blade."

"You're freaking sexy, Mrs. Kiarra Blade!"

Kiarra

Relaxing on their private patio days later, Kiarra laid beside her husband on the lounger. From their reclining positions, they had a great view of the resort.

Steps led from one of the outdoor pools straight into a relaxation spot where a crescent-shaped cream couch fenced with black stones sat like a throne in the main pool. The couch, decorated with matching round cushions featured small black nesting tables to hold food. On their right side, a floating deck held over a dozen seats and tables, the site of the fancy a la carte restaurant where they'd had their lunch on many occasions. And across from the floating couch, coconut trees stood in rows in their glorious heights in the distance, their palm leaves seemed to whisper sweet nothing to the blue sky above.

"When would you say we first met?" she asked her husband, deciding to come clean at last.

"Officially?" He shrugged. "At the barbecue party."

Her eyes almost cracked with shock, so she sat up. "What do you mean *officially*? Did we meet before that, Ryder?"

He gave her that cute wink that melted her heart any day.

"Yeah. Sort of behind the scenes."

"Ryder, what are you talking about?"

"I saw you at the trash site a couple of times."

Surprised, she squealed, grabbed one patterned cushion and hit his chest. "Why did you never mention it? I thought it was my own little secret."

"Ow! You want to pillow fight, babe?"

Laughing, he carried her over his shoulder, marched inside, dumped her on the couch and snatched one pillow.

"What do you mean your *own little secret*? Did you think you saw me and I didn't see you, hmm?"

Charging forward, Ryder knocked her arm with the pillow and hers flew out of her fingers.

"Yeah!" Feeling battle ready, she snatched the pillow again and knocked his shoulder. "I took the time to study your features. It was my moment."

"Your *moment*? I went to take out trash. Then I see this woman lurking in the shadows. You didn't want to be seen, and I didn't want to chat. I'd say it worked out well for both of us at the time."

"But you pretended you'd never seen me, husband!"

"You did the same, wife!"

He bashed her thigh with the pillow.

Giggling, she fought back, knocking his head and receiving his battering with the pillow in return.

"Because I didn't want you to know I'd seen you."

"Why, stalker?" he mocked, sticking out his tongue.

"Maybe I stalked you a bit," she admitted, taking her turn to batter his abs with her pillow.

"You think? I'd say it was a lot and I enjoyed it."

Her husband pried the pillow from her fingers and pinned her down on the couch with his body. When she opened her mouth to speak, he stroked her lips with his mouth and slipped his tongue inside. While she kissed him back, he kneaded her entrance before thrusting inside her. He ground his hips against hers and bowed to suck her breast.

Wonderful!

A thousand explosions rang through her as she also jammed her hips to meet his own. She leaned forward to kiss his nipple one after the other. For as long as it took, he showed her in the most intimate way how much he loved her. With their arms twined around each other after they both shuddered for minutes, she rested her head on his shoulder.

"Ryder Blade, I longed for you from the start." It was the perfect time to tell him how she felt.

"In my heart, in my soul and in my body, I'm yours. Forever, I'll always long for you, Kia."

Sleepy-eyed now, Kiarra pressed her mouth to his chest. "So, do you regret saying, *not in a million years* to my audacious marriage proposal at the barbecue party?"

"Without a doubt, Mrs. Kiarra Blade. I sincerely apologize for turning you down."

Giggling quietly, she nodded. "I told you so."

Ryder cuddled her in his arms, her forever home.

Over the duration of their four-week honeymoon stay at *Stella Island Luxury Resort & Spa*, Ryder and Kiarra toured the white sandy beaches, discovered the wild nature, climbed the majestic mountains and surfed across the twinkling ocean waters.

Later – Thank You

On their first wedding anniversary, Kiarra Blade had a baby girl to the delight of her husband, Ryder. With the arrival of the baby, nobody recalled Kiarra's long and challenging thirty-six-hour labour.

Surrounded by their families in the private ward, the excited couple named their chubby-faced, dark-haired beauty, *Kiesha Wilma Diamond Blade*. The ruby-cheek baby was the cynosure of all eyes. Everyone jostled to catch a glimpse of Keisha whose first instinct was to fight to push her cute fist past her pink lips.

When Keisha let out a helpless shriek, Ryder intervened. He carried his new born from his sister-in-law, Jalicia and placed her across his wife's boobs.

Beaming, despite her fatigue, Kiarra Blade welcomed Keisha with a soft cooing sound as she wrapped her arms around their blessing from God. Smiling, Kiarra eased her huge darkened nipple into the baby's parted lips. As quickly as the baby's yelling started, it stopped.

"Congratulations Kiarra! Ryder!" Lindsay Blade and Alana Watson chirped.

"We're so blessed! Thanks be to God, who blesses us with good gifts and adds no sorrow." Nolan and Mabel Wright praised God, pulling their hands together in prayer and raising choruses.

They all sang, laughed and hugged Ryder in turn.

Free from the round of family hugs at last, Ryder leaned across his wife and kissed her temple. With his fingers, he brushed her sweat-soaked dark curls back and kissed her lips.

"You're my beautiful queen, Kiarra Wright. Our daughter's gorgeous, just like you. I love you more."

"Thank you, honey." She clasped her fingers around his arm. "Thank God for safe delivery and for Keisha. I'm so happy we've got a daughter."

"We're a family now, babe," he gushed, hugging his wife and his baby as his heart pounded with explosive joy and love.

When Keisha turned three, Ryder and Kiarra Blade started a non-profit organization named after their daughter. They built a youth centre in Downtown San Diego, California where Ryder gave motivational speeches to children in foster care, street kids and errant youths engaged in community service. At the forum, Ryder often shared his personal story.

By so doing, Ryder and his wife, Kiarra helped save many children with their NGO initiative and by being good role models in their community.

Within five years, Ryder expanded *Rich Earth Coffee* to three countries in Europe. In the long term, he also planned to grow his business to Australia.

On their sixth wedding anniversary, Ryder and Kiarra had a healthy, gorgeous baby boy named *Romeo Kadesh Blade*. It was a celebration of love for their entire families and friends. Taking centre stage, five-year old Keisha Wilma Diamond was the happiest child around, cuddling her baby brother like she did with the latest and cutest toy in San Diego.

Meanwhile, Alana and Alex Watson had a baby boy about five months before Keisha was born. They named him, *Brenden Mark Watson*.

Jalicia and Leron Jackson also had a baby boy the same month Kiarra and Ryder Blade's daughter, Keisha turned six months. They named him, *D'Sean Benjamin Jackson*.

Deiondre Wright and Teona Lewis went out for their scheduled drink date and dated officially for several months. Eager to get introduced to his girlfriend, Kiarra and Ryder organized a family get-together for the newly-dating couple, inviting their family and friends.

After dating for six months however, Deiondre and Teona took a break, citing pressure of work for their separation. Kiarra and Ryder as well as Jalicia and Leron were quite disappointed about the split.

On a happier note, Ryder eventually set up, Jerrad and Madison and the pair started dating. On his part, Jerrad is hopeful things would work out with Madison, so he could settle down like his bro.

Also, Taleisha got the shock of her life when Jevonte, the guy she had been working to get his attention for months asked her out on a dinner date. With many things in common and with the fact they enjoy each other's company, the duo hopes their relationship would continue to deepen over the coming months.

Names & Meanings

Kiarra – Light, fortunate
Wright – Worker of wood
Ryder – Knight, mounted warrior
Blade – Wealthy glory
Mabel – Beautiful, loving
Nolan – To shout
Jalicia – Honest, benevolent
Deiondre – Valley
Leron – My son
Lindsay – A lake
Alana – Precious, child
Alexander – Defender of men
Taleisha – Blooming life
Zachary – The Lord has remembered
Jerrad – Rules by the spear
Hailey – Wood, meadow
Jamie – Supplanter
Duane – Meadow
Madison – Battle mighty
Nicole – Victory of the people
Teona – Divine

The End

Thank you so much for buying and reading
Longing for You.
*Please post a review. I can't wait to read your
comments.*

More Books from Stella

~ Flirty & Feisty Romance Novels ~

Scroll down to find other books by Stella in eBook & Paperback formats.

Irresistible Driver

https://amzn.to/2ukcM5s

"Unwrap me if you can and at your own risk!" Running from his pain, a seasoned bachelor has a row with his assigned sexy female driver who might just show him what he needs to relieve his aching heart and body.

◇ ◇ ◇ ◇

Christmas Desire:

https://amzn.to/2O6cWo6

She is a passionate lawyer and he is a reckless billionaire. His desire is to fall into bed with her. Her desire is to stay the heck away from him. But their banter is sarcastic and their passion is electric.

◇ ◇ ◇ ◇

Tempted by the Princess ~ 1 & 2
https://amzn.to/2LOTuwl
& https://amzn.to/2Ot8IcK

When an elegant woman who knows her way around the boardroom and bedroom finds herself torn between duty and her heart, she is at the mercy of a complete stranger who wants to show her what she is missing.

◇ ◇ ◇ ◇

Hooked by one Curvy Girl ~ 1 & 2
https://amzn.to/2XQOoTN
& https://amzn.to/2XSABuw

The moment curvy Nollywood actress–who does not date single guys–gets turned down by one mysteriously sexy, tattooed single guy she asked to be her paid plus-one for one night, her chest tightens as he stirs lust between her thick thigh.

◇ ◇ ◇ ◇

Naughty Promise:
https://amzn.to/2XOe2qF

Lonely nights switch to sweet dreams when her new staff catches her eye and drives her out of her mind with an aching need, she must control even if it kills her.

◇ ◇ ◇ ◇

Christmas Seduction:
https://amzn.to/2GACfdg

Engaged and happy, one CEO has his family Christmas holiday in chaos when his employee, an unruly female pilot with smoky eyes, a wide smile and a figure that catches his breath sticks her mouth and presence in the wrong places. Why can't she follow his rules?

◇ ◇ ◇ ◇

Irresistible Passion:
https://amzn.to/2XLMNNx

When a single-dad who lives a double life sneaks inside his mansion in Atlanta & finds a woman with full curves, sun-kissed lips & long dark hair asleep on his sofa, all hell breaks loose. Who is she & what does she want?

◇ ◇ ◇ ◇

"Shocking Affair":
https://amzn.to/2XR4RWr

Although the female CEO of Hotshot Publishers resists the awareness burning between herself and the janitor, things get out of control after she assigns him to clean her office.

◇ ◇ ◇ ◇

Guilty of Love:
http://amzn.to/2C8q9DW

A quick holiday turns into a fairy-tale romance when his eyes clashes with hers at the airport, only to find out she is from the same family he swore to hate.

◇ ◇ ◇ ◇

Your Christmas Gift:
http://amzn.to/2nE95nc

Expecting to be alone at Christmas, she strolls inside the penthouse suite to find one drop-dead gorgeous, tattooed man lying on the sofa sporting only hip-hugging boxers and a brutal tongue.

◇ ◇ ◇ ◇

All of Me:
http://amzn.to/2zHluJq

He will stop at nothing to get close to his pretty next-door neighbour, but he does not expect to involve his heart, just his head.

◇ ◇ ◇ ◇

"You're Mine":
http://amzn.to/2uJBGHA

Pregnant or not, the stubborn woman who lives under his mom's roof and causes a stir in his heart and head has questions to answer.

◇ ◇ ◇ ◇

Enticed Forever:
http://amzn.to/2qvkCGf

When one famous bad-boy tycoon meets a woman–who wants nothing money can buy–he is not prepared for the body-popping tension which grips his chest and sweeps him off his feet.

◇ ◇ ◇ ◇

Naked Attraction:

http://amzn.to/2lwDRcv

A hot and sexy Café owner tempts and pursues a feisty female District Judge until she submits in his bed.

◇ ◇ ◇ ◇

Indecent:

http://amzn.to/2bUNpvH

Her plans change when one gorgeous property developer pays her to stay in his home for the holidays.

◇ ◇ ◇ ◇

His Ring:

http://amzn.to/2bEafdn

After denying her attraction for her gardener for good reasons, she finds out she can't stop thinking about the man who has her emotions upside down.

◇ ◇ ◇ ◇

Forbidden Dance ~ Book 1 &

http://amzn.to/1UVQw7u
Red Velvet Rose ~ Book 2
http://amzn.to/25KW34c

After she abandons her cheating husband's London home and dances her way into the heart of a new admirer in Casablanca, her life changes in more ways than one.

Red Velvet Rose:

Ruggedly-handsome car dealer who still nurses a broken heart spills coffee on a woman in the café, only to get himself tangled in more ways than one.

◇ ◇ ◇ ◇

Tempting Desire:
http://amzn.to/23hbulS

A sexy business man has set rules—not to mix business with pleasure—until he meets a tempting woman who is a hard nut to crack.

◇ ◇ ◇ ◇

Seduced Hearts:
http://amzn.to/1qzozTj

When an old friend stops over at their home before Christmas, one married couple gets more trouble than they imagined.

◇ ◇ ◇ ◇

Wild Whispers:
http://amzn.to/23ZuTD1

When handsome photographer finds an abandoned shelter, he has no idea his heart is about to flip over with a woman who has a dark past.

◇ ◇ ◇ ◇

Lust:
http://amzn.to/2fUIWfh

When he appears on her doorstep looking drop-dead gorgeous and oh-so-sexy, she knows her secret must stay guarded or risk losing everything.

◇ ◇ ◇ ◇

Love at Christmas:
http://amzn.to/2fz3PwE

The second she is paired up with one mysterious guest, their attraction is instant and the urge to kiss him is strong. But there is more to him than meets the eyes.

◇ ◇ ◇ ◇

Husband to Rent:
http://amzn.to/1SisexH

Fascinated by the sexy antics of the woman who offers to take his mind off his worries, he forgets his plan to keep their dealings straight.

◇ ◇ ◇ ◇

Stolen Valentine Kiss ~ Book 1 &
http://amzn.to/23hbJgP
Kiss My Lips ~ Book 2:

http://amzn.to/1qbgnLp

Running away from a heartbreak throws her on the lap of charming New Jersey Publisher who steals a kiss from her lips on Valentine's night.

Kiss My Lips:

An attractive publisher who is engaged, has his wedding plans turning upside down so fast, he will need a miracle, if he wants to say, 'I do' and kiss his bride's lips at the altar.

◇ ◇ ◇ ◇

Stolen Kisses: Holiday Series Books 1 & 2:
http://amzn.to/1Wh0zmR

A super-sexy New Jersey Publisher with no intention to have an affair, finds his heart trouble after a stolen kiss on Valentine's night.

◇ ◇ ◇ ◇

Royal Cowries ~ Book 1 &
http://amzn.to/1qz0Vtc
His Choice ~ Book 2
http://amzn.to/2dZzPFJ

She is in a dilemma—to become a trophy wife to a man old enough to be her father or end up in the arms of a stranger.

His Choice:

It was a simple task—to capture a new kingdom and its treasures and get rewarded. But things get complicated when she meets the handsome prince who is ready to give his life to save his people.

Social Media Links

Please keep in touch with all ***Flirty & Feisty*** Romance Novel new releases & promotions and also get advice on relationships, on writing and read juicy excerpts on my Blog.

Follow me on Facebook

Facebook

Be my friend on Goodreads

Goodreads

Follow me on Twitter

Twitter

Find my posts on

Google+

Find my Pins on Pinterest

Pinterest